jQuery and jQuery UI

JAY BLANCHARD

D1239876

Peachpit Press

Visual QuickStart Guide
jQuery and jQuery UI
Jay Blanchard

Peachpit Press
www.peachpit.com.

To report errors, please send a note to errata@peachpit.com.
Peachpit Press is a division of Pearson Education.

Copyright © 2013 by Jay Blanchard

Acquisitions and Project Editor: Rebecca Gulick
Developmental Editor: Dave Awl
Copy Editor: Liz Welch
Technical Reviewer: Jesse Castro
Production Coordinator: Myrna Vladic
Compositor: David Van Ness
Proofreader: Patricia Pane
Indexer: Valerie Haynes Perry
Cover Design: RHDG / Riezebos Holzbaur Design Group, Peachpit Press
Interior Design: Peachpit Press
Logo Design: MINE™ www.minesf.com

ISBN-13:   978-0-321-88514-2
ISBN-10:   0-321-88514-7

9 8 7 6 5 4 3 2 1

Printed and bound in the United States of America

Dedication

Dedicated to the memory of Mr. Coy Watkins, who instilled a love of science and exploration in hundreds of students...especially me.

Special Thanks to:

It is not possible to embark upon the journey of creating a book without a lot of talented and supportive people by your side. I love that they get me, warts and all, even if it means that I say, "I can't...I have to write."

To my daughters Brittany and Kaitlyn, thank you for inspiring me and cheering me on. You make life worth every single moment. I love you to the moon and back...infinity!

To my Dad, I could not be here without the life lessons, support, and love that you have so graciously shared with a hardheaded kid. Thank you for being my Dad. I love you.

To Rebecca Gulick, the journey gets more interesting as we go. Thank you for your patient and firm guidance while maintaining a sense of humor. You're truly a treasure.

To Dave Awl, thank you for steering the boat through some choppy seas. You've taught me a lot about that.

To Jesse Castro, what can I say? Your depth and breadth of knowledge always astounds me. Your ability to keep me on point is amazing. Your friendship and quirky sense of humor make me smile. Thank you!

To the Peachpit/Pearson team, thank you for your patience and your ability to turn sows' ears into silk purses. Your wow factor is way off the top of the scale.

To my valued mentor Larry Ullman, you know how to cut to the heart of the matter and remind me what the value of humbleness is.

To my friends who have supported me and carried me through when the pressure was on and time was short, I appreciate you beyond the mere measure of words on a page.

To the jQuery team and community, thank you for your dedication to bringing a great product to the masses, your encouragement, and your steadfast vision of what a JavaScript library should look like. Your willingness to share your knowledge and to bring people into the fold is tremendously valuable and welcomed.

Contents at a Glance

Table of Contents

Introduction

Welcome to jQuery!

You are on the verge of learning how to add the world's most popular JavaScript library to your websites and web applications. You'll be joining the ranks of developers for companies like Google, ESPN, and Best Buy in applying jQuery to your web development arsenal.

Originally developed in 2005 by John Resig, the jQuery library has grown into a mature and powerful tool for enhancing web pages. Developers worldwide took up the banner and began developing widgets (called plugins) using the jQuery library for the foundation. The jQuery group joined in the plugin craze, absorbing some very popular plugins into its framework and adding some widgets to an additional library, jQuery UI, in 2007.

Since that time, the jQuery Foundation has continued to enhance and rework the library to make it more robust and efficient. New versions of the library with new features and enhancements are rolled out at an incredible pace to keep up with the changing landscape of web development.

Why Use This Book?

The goal of this book is to introduce you to the concepts of the jQuery and jQuery UI libraries, as well as how to use those concepts in practical examples. You'll be able to use the concepts right away in your web projects.

What Is jQuery?

There is a very simple answer to that question: jQuery is JavaScript. To be more specific, jQuery is a free, open source library of code written in the JavaScript programming language.

Because jQuery is JavaScript, it can take advantage of many of JavaScript's functions and concepts, like object notation, and in many cases make them easier to work with.

At the heart of jQuery is its selector engine, Sizzle, which is also written in JavaScript. The Sizzle selector engine makes it easy to use CSS (Cascading Style Sheet) selectors as jQuery objects to work with specific web page elements or groups of elements.

Variables and functions and arguments, oh my!

If this is your first foray into programming languages, let's cover some of the basic concepts of putting together a working piece of software. You'll see examples of these concepts in nearly every exercise.

The first concept is that of variables. Variables are essentially containers for pieces of information that can come in the form of values, arrays (indexed collections of items), or objects (items that have a collection of properties). The following will declare a variable and set its value to be blank:

```
var myVariable = '';
var myNewVariable = '';
```

Learning jQuery

Learning how to use jQuery is an organic process. For example, knowing how to create selectors is no fun if you don't do something with the items you select.

You'll be introduced early on to many of jQuery's methods and functions even if the concept has not yet been covered in the book. You'll be guided to chapters where more information concerning those methods and functions can be found at the end of each exercise.

Starting in Chapter 2, "Handling Events," you'll begin building jQuery functions within the framework of a website's templates. Once complete, the web pages will have used very many of the jQuery methods available, including some of the jQuery UI plugin widgets (widgets and plugins are small, stand-alone tools that are easily added to websites). The markup and code for the completed web pages (including the PHP and MySQL queries) are provided for you in Appendix B, "An Active jQuery Website."

All of the code used in the book is available for download from www.jayblanchard.net. Just look for the jQuery and jQuery UI Visual QuickStart Guide download link.

The variable is now ready to be used, and you can populate it with any value that you need just by referring to it:

```
myVariable = 1234;

myNewVariable = $('#id');
```

One thing that you'll need to be aware of with variables: They have a scope. In other words, a variable may only be available within the confines of a function and not available anywhere else in your code. JavaScript variable scope has been a popular topic of discussion, and you'll find many good references online.

TIP Give your variables and functions meaningful names, because doing so will help you maintain your code later as well as provide clues for how the variable or function is used.

The next concept is designed for testing a condition and then reacting to that condition. Conditional statements come in the form of **if** (if this, then that) or **while** (while condition exists, do this):

```
if(myNewVariable == 1234) {
    // then do this
} else {
    // then do that
}
```

The **while** condition typically starts a loop (there is also a **for** condition that sets up a loop). Here you'll test the value of **myVariable**, print out the value of the variable, and then reduce the variable's value by 1. The loop will run as long as **myVariable**'s value is greater than 0.

```
var myVariable = 10;

while(myVariable > 0) {
    // do something
    document.write(myVariable +
"<br>");
    myVariable--;
}
```

A little more difficult concept is the function. A *function* is typically a group of instructions that allow you to perform a set of actions just by calling the function name. Then you can return the result of the function's actions.

To declare a function, you do this:

```
function myFunction() {
    // place instructions here
    var result = 1 + 1; //
     instruction
    return result;
}
```

continues on next page

To use the function, you might do something like this:

```
var myVariable = myFunction();
    //myVariable now equals 2
```

Sometimes you'll want to send information to a function. This is known as passing arguments. Revamp your function to look like this:

```
function myFunction(argument) {
    var result = argument + 1;
    return result;
}
```

Now you can pass an argument to the function:

```
var myVariable = 5;
var myNewVariable =
    myFunction(myVariable);
```

You pass **myVariable** to **myFunction**. Then **myVariable** becomes **argument**. You add 1 to **argument** and return the result. **myNewVariable** is now equal to 6 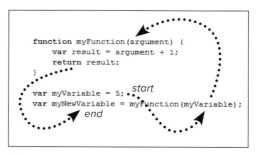.

Functions are great when you need to perform the same action over and over again while maybe passing different arguments. You can also set up functions to receive and process multiple arguments. Functions will become a key tool in your development toolbox.

This is nowhere near an exhaustive introduction to programming, but it should be enough to get your feet wet and give you the understanding that you need to work through the jQuery exercises in the book. There are many good resources for learning how to program with JavaScript and many other languages where the concepts are the same, only the syntax is changed.

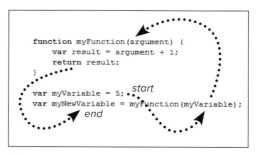

```
function myFunction(argument) {
    var result = argument + 1;
    return result;
}

var myVariable = 5;    start
var myNewVariable = myFunction(myVariable);
                       end
```

Ⓐ The transformation of an argument.

Functions or Methods?

One concept that may be a little vague is the difference between functions and methods. It seems, on the surface, that they're the same thing. In reality they are not.

A *function* is a piece of code that's called by name. You can pass data to a function and the function will operate on that data. You can also return data from a function. Any data passed to the function is passed explicitly—you choose to pass data to a function.

A *method* is a piece of code that is normally associated with an object, like when a selector is bound to a jQuery method. You still call a method by name, and in most respects, it's identical to a function except for two key differences: A method is implicitly passed the object for which it was called and the method is able to operate on data that's contained within the object.

The water becomes muddy when you begin to understand that functions may contain methods and in a similar fashion you may create methods, like jQuery plugins and extensions, that contain functions. If you remember how information is passed, either explicitly or implicitly, you'll be able to keep the differences straight.

Learning the Basics

In many cases, your first decision as a web developer using jQuery is deciding whether to download the jQuery core to make it available from your web server or use a hosted service known as a CDN (Content Delivery Network). Both have advantages and disadvantages.

The single largest advantage of using a CDN, like Google's, is that its distributed network almost always uses servers closest to the website visitor to deliver the jQuery library. Once the library from a CDN is cached by the browser, it doesn't have to be downloaded again (as long as the browser cache isn't cleared), which makes site loading faster. The largest disadvantage is that you'll have to rely on a third party to be available when your site is requested by a first-time visitor.

If you decide to host the jQuery library yourself, your biggest advantage is that you'll be in control. If someone can reach your site, they can get all of the files needed to use your site. Once it's cached from your site, returning visitors gain the same advantage they'd get if you were using a CDN. You can also create jQuery applications that require no connection to the Internet if the application has no requirement for a remote data source. The biggest disadvantage is that some browsers limit the number of connections they can make to a server simultaneously, so getting everything downloaded quickly may be difficult.

For most people in this day and age bandwidth is not a concern, but you may want to consider those do who have bandwidth limitations or who are using browsers that place low limits on connections to servers.

Your best bet may be using a CDN with a fallback to a local (on your web server) copy of the jQuery library. Let's prepare for creating a fallback by downloading a copy of jQuery first.

To download jQuery from jquery.com:

1. Open a browser and visit jquery.com .

2. Choose the version of jQuery you'd like to download, either production or development. The production version is minified (white spaces and comments stripped) to provide the smallest possible footprint and overhead.

3. The jQuery file will appear in your browser **B**.

4. Save the file to your computer and then move it to the proper place on your web server.

TIP In order to facilitate offline development, you'll want to download a copy of jQuery to host on your local machine.

A The jQuery website. The links to download the code are in the upper-right-hand corner of the site.

B The raw JavaScript code for the jQuery library.

Once you've downloaded the file, you can include it in your web projects. Let's set up a fallback method to use with Google's CDN.

To use jQuery in your projects:

- Add the following code within the `<head></head>` tags in your web pages:

```
<script type="text/javascript"
  src="https://ajax.googleapis.com/
  ajax/libs/jquery/1.7.2/jquery.
  min.js">

</script>

<script type="text/javascript">

if (typeof jQuery ==
  'undefined') {

document.write(unescape("%3Cscript
  src='path/to/jquery-1.7.2.min.js'
  type='text/javascript'%3E%3C/
  script%3E"));

}

</script>
```

The first script is an attempt to include the jQuery core in your web project from the CDN. The second script then tests to see if the jQuery object is available. If the jQuery object isn't available, a line is written to the HTML file to load the jQuery file from the local source.

TIP If you're using HTML5, it isn't necessary to include the type attribute in your script tags.

TIP You have choices when it comes to CDNs. Microsoft, Google, and jQuery all offer CDNs.

Minifying your code

As you're developing your markup, style sheets, and jQuery code, you'll leave a lot of whitespace, tabs, and comments in your files to make the files easy to maintain and read. This is great during development, but for production you should consider minifying your code.

The process of minifying code removes all of the unnecessary whitespace, comments, and formatting characters, which makes the download of the code much faster. Some minifying applications will even check your code for errors and perform other actions to reduce your code to the smallest possible size without losing functionality.

My favorite application for minifying code is the Google Closure Compiler .

To minify your code with the Google Closure Compiler:

1. Go to http://closure-compiler.appspot.com/home to access the application.

2. Modify the line of code in the left-hand pane of the compiler containing the directive **@output_file_name**. Use the name of the file you wish to save your minified code to:

   `// ==ClosureCompiler==`

   `// @compilation_level`
   `→ WHITESPACE_ONLY`

   `// @output_file_name`
   `→ jquery.custom.min.js`

   `// ==/ClosureCompiler==`

3. Copy your jQuery code into the space below the directives.

4. Click the Compile button in the upper-left pane of the compiler.

C The Google Closure Compiler interface.

Once you've completed those steps, you'll see the compiled code in the right pane of the application. In the upper-right section of the interface, you can get statistics about the original size of the code, followed by the compiled size of the code to give you an idea of how much compression occurred.

Also in the upper-right section of the compiler is a link to your minified code, using the name you specified in the directives. Clicking on the link will open your raw, minified JavaScript code in your browser window. Save the code to your computer and move it to the proper location on your web server.

TIP Always keep a development version of your code containing all of the comments and whitespace for readability and minify only for your production environment.

Performing Progressive Enhancement

One of the major benefits of using the jQuery library is that you can use it on any website without having to modify any of your HTML or CSS.

Most websites are developed using a similar workflow. The HTML markup and CSS are developed first along with any artwork to give the website its look and feel. Once complete, the website may be fully functioning. Most developers keep their style sheets separate from their markup, choosing to include the CSS in their projects via link tags in the head of HTML documents. It's just good organization. Maintenance is easier and much more efficient.

Because jQuery has the ability to interact with the full range of CSS selectors and HTML elements, it can be kept apart from the markup, whereas many JavaScript calls have to be written inline with the markup. For instance, to capture a click event from a link tag you'd have to include a call to JavaScript's `onClick()` method within the anchor tag:

```
<a href="some.html"
→ onClick="jsFunction">
```

It can be a lot of work to go back to a website you've developed to add JavaScript interaction.

TIP When planning new websites and applications that you'll be using jQuery on, be sure to add classes and IDs that will assist you in the development process.

With jQuery you'd include your jQuery file in a script tag, just as you did with the jQuery core earlier in "Learning the Basics." Then you could write the click event handler into your jQuery code file:

```
$('a[href="some.html"]').click(...
```

This means you never have to touch your existing markup. The concept of keeping everything separate is known as *progressive enhancement*.

The basic rules for progressive enhancement are simple. Develop your markup, add your styles, and then enhance with jQuery—with each of those being in stand-alone files. In Chapter 1, "Using Selectors," progressive enhancement isn't used—all of the HTML, CSS, and jQuery (except the jQuery core) you'll write are in one file. This was done for simplicity's sake. Once you start developing jQuery in earnest (beginning with Chapter 2, "Handling Events"), the markup, styles, and jQuery code are kept in separate files and included in the HTML as needed.

Tracking Down Tools

All you need other than the jQuery core file is a good text editor. Every developer has his or her preferences, so I'm going to give you a couple of recommendations. I encourage you to experiment with a few different text editors until you find one you're comfortable with. Additionally, **Table I.1** contains some recommendations for other tools that will help you to become a better jQuery developer and a better web developer.

As your skills and abilities grow, you may find that other tools will enhance your workflow and make your development process more efficient.

Rewind and Review

Take a few moments to reflect on what you've learned in this introduction:

- Where do you get the jQuery library?
- Is it better to host your own jQuery code or rely on a Content Delivery Network (CDN)?
- What is jQuery?
- What is the advantage of progressive enhancement?

TABLE I.1 Suggested Tools

Name	Information
Eclipse IDE	General-purpose text editor for Windows or Mac. Available from www.eclipse.org.
Sublime Text 2	General-purpose text editor for Windows, Mac, and Linux. Available from www.sublimetext.com.
Firebug	DOM inspector and troubleshooting tools for Firefox on Windows and Mac. Available from http://getfirebug.com.
Developer Tools	DOM inspector and troubleshooting tools available with Internet Explorer 9 on Windows. Just press F12.
Developer Tools	DOM inspector and troubleshooting tools for Google Chrome. It comes bundled with Chrome: Select Tools > Developer Tools.
XAMPP	A personal web server you can install on your computer for local development. Includes PHP and MySQL, and runs on Windows. Available from www.apachefriends.org.
MAMP	A personal web server you can install on your Mac. Includes PHP and MySQL. Available from www.mamp.info.

1

Using Selectors

One of the strengths of the jQuery library is that it gives you the ability to easily select and interact with Document Object Model (DOM) elements in your web pages.

The selectors will be familiar to you if you've done any web development with Cascading Style Sheets (CSS), because jQuery's selector syntax is nearly a duplicate of the selectors you'd use when preparing style properties for your websites. jQuery makes use of the Sizzle JavaScript CSS selector engine, which was developed by John Resig, the creator of jQuery. The jQuery library also adds several specific selector extensions to enhance the library's syntax and make the library easier to use.

In this chapter, you'll learn how to choose and use jQuery's selectors to gain control over DOM elements as well as groups of elements in your web pages. You'll also learn how to combine selectors and then apply filters to your selectors for greater flexibility and control.

In This Chapter

Using Basic Selectors

Although jQuery provides a host of selector options, you'll find yourself using one of the basic selectors (element, id, or class) most of the time. **Table 1.1** lists the basic selectors and what they do.

As you're creating the markup for your web pages, you should plan classes and IDs carefully. Good planning will make your life much easier when you get ready to apply jQuery to your website. It's easy to get tripped up and wonder why your jQuery code isn't working when you don't keep your **id**s unique or you fail to define them properly. In HTML5, most of the restrictions on IDs have been relaxed. You can use any character in an ID and it must contain at least one character, but each ID within a web page must be unique. If you have two elements with the same ID, you may get odd results when applying jQuery code to those elements and the results may differ from browser to browser.

When you wish to add jQuery code designed to have an effect on a group of elements, I recommend you use classes

Using IDs and Classes

If you're new to web development, you may not be familiar with the concept of IDs and classes in HTML markup and CSS.

In HTML, an ID is an attribute that is assigned to an element by placing **id="id_name"** (where **id_name** is unique for every element assigned an ID) within the element tag. For example, you might assign an ID to a paragraph element like this: **<p id="paragraph_1">**. In your CSS you would refer to the ID by placing a hash mark (**#**) in front of the ID's name: **#paragraph_1**.

On the other hand, you may assign the same class to any number of elements. For instance, **class="redline"** can be assigned to any element. In CSS, you would address a class by placing a period in front of the name: **.redline**.

With jQuery, you use the same syntax used in CSS, prefixing IDs with the hash mark and prefixing classes with a period (**.**).

TABLE 1.1 Basic Selectors

Selector Name	What It Does
all $('*')	Selects every element within a web page, beginning with the body element. The **all** selector is rarely used and can be slow if the web page contains a large number of elements.
element $('element')	Selects all of this element type, such as **div**, **p**, or **h1**.
id $('#id_name')	Selects the one element in a web page having the ID. The ID must be preceded with a hash or pound sign. (Each ID in a web page must be unique!)
class $('.class_name')	Selects all elements having a particular class. Class names are preceded by a period.

for those elements. First of all, it's usually easier to remember named groups, and second, you can apply jQuery methods to all sorts of elements that have the same class. Judicious use of classes gives you tremendous flexibility when it comes to designing your jQuery interactions.

To use the basic selectors:

1. Open **basic_html5.html**, the basic HTML5 template described in Appendix B, in your favorite text editor or integrated development environment (IDE) 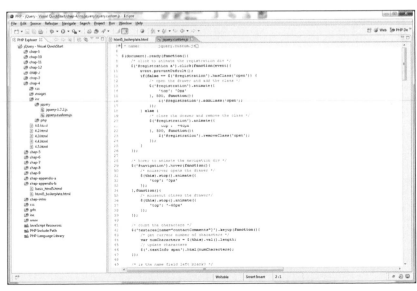, or open Script **1.1.html** to follow along.

2. Place the following markup in the body of the HTML page:

```
<h1>Header 1</h1>

<p id="introduction">Lorem ipsum
→ dolor sit amet, consectetur
→ adipiscing elit. </p>

<h2>Header 2</h2>
```

```
<p class="content">Nulla ut
→ Auctor dui. Duis ultricies
→ eros faucibus neque aliquet
→ vel tempus sem tincidunt.
→ </p>

<p class="content">Integer eget
→ tellus nec diam pellentesque
→ cursus. Nulla facilisi. </p>

<p class="content">Curabitur
→ dictum tortor vitae nulla
→ vehicula sed porta tellus
→ porta.</p>
```

I used the popular pseudo-Latin "Lorem ipsum…" for filler here. Please feel free to use whatever text you would like.

continues on next page

A I like to work in the Eclipse IDE because it allows me to easily organize a project.

3. Add this jQuery code to the head section of your page directly underneath where you included the jQuery core library **B**:

```
<script type="text/javascript">
$(document).ready(function(){
$( '*' ).css({ 'border': '1px
    solid #FF0000', 'margin':'5px',
    'padding': '5px' });
$( 'h1' ).css({ 'background':
    '#FFFF00' });
$( '.content' ).css({ 'font-
    style': 'italic'});
$( '#introduction' ).css({
    'color': '#0000FF' });
});
</script>
```

4. Save the new file as **basic.html**, place it in your web directory, and load it into your web browser **C**.

These examples used the jQuery **css()** method to apply styles to each of the selectors. The **css()** method is flexible and allows you to style elements on your web pages quickly and easily. You'll learn more about the CSS methods in Chapter 6, "Traversing the DOM Tree."

TIP Plan the use of your ids and classes well. This will make adding interactive elements with jQuery much easier.

TIP Use the all selector sparingly; it can slow down your browser, especially when your web page includes a lot of elements.

TIP To improve performance, especially if you're going to use the same selector over and over again, you can cache selectors by placing them in variables. For instance, `var cachedSelector = $('selected elements');` places all of the selected elements in the variable `cachedSelector`, which can then be used in your jQuery function calls, as in this example: `cachedSelector.css({...});`.

```
1  <!DOCTYPE html>
2  <html>
3    <head>
4      <meta charset="UTF-8">
5      <title>jQuery Visual QuickStart</title>
6
7      <!-- jquery & javascript -->
8      <script type="text/javascript" src="../inc/jquery-1.7.2.js"></script>
9      <script type="text/javascript">
10 ➡   $(document).ready(function(){
11         $( '*' ).css({ 'border': '1px solid #FF0000', 'margin':'5px', 'padding': '5px' });
12         $( 'h1' ).css({ 'background': '#FFFF00' });
13         $( '.content' ).css({ 'font-style': 'italic'});
14         $( '#introduction' ).css({ 'color': '#0000FF' });
15       });
16      </script>
17    </head>
18    <body>
19      <h1>Header 1</h1>
20        <p id="introduction">Lorem ipsum dolor sit amet, consectetur adipiscing elit. </p>
21      <h2>Header 2</h2>
22        <p class="content">Nulla ut auctor dui. Duis ultricies eros faucibus neque aliquet vel tempu
23        <p class="content">Integer eget tellus nec diam pellentesque cursus. Nulla facilisi. </p>
24        <p class="content">Curabitur dictum tortor vitae nulla vehicula sed porta tellus porta. </p>
25    </body>
26  </html>
```

B The arrow shows where you should add the jQuery code to the page.

Header 1
Lorem ipsum dolor sit amet, consectetur adipiscing elit.
Header 2
Nulla ut auctor dui. Duis ultricies eros faucibus neque aliquet vel tempus sem tincidunt.
Integer eget tellus nec diam pellentesque cursus. Nulla facilisi.
Curabitur dictum tortor vitae nulla vehicula sed porta tellus porta.

C Your completed web page with styles applied using jQuery's basic selectors and the **css()** method.

D The style now applies to all **h1** and **h2** elements.

Combining selectors

When using jQuery, you can combine selectors just as you can when writing CSS. Combining selectors has a number of benefits, including shortening your coding time and keeping your code neater—with the added benefit of creating less code for the browser to download and parse. Smaller load times equate to less overhead and more efficient web applications.

You can combine all the jQuery selectors where it makes sense as you're creating your web application, just as you would when combining those selectors in CSS.

To combine selectors:

1. Open the **basic.html** file in your text editor or follow along in Script **1.2.html**.

2. Locate the following line of jQuery code:

```
$( 'h1' ).css({ 'background':
    '#FFFF00' });
```

3. Change the selector to add **h2** elements:

```
$( 'h1, h2' )
```

Be sure to include a comma between each element.

4. Save the file as **combined.html** and load into your web browser. All of the header elements in the page now have the same style **D**.

> **TIP** If you find yourself combining lots of selectors, it will be better and more efficient just to add a class to those elements. This will help keep your selector shorter and easier to keep track of.

Applying Filters to Selectors

The jQuery library offers a number of filters that allow you to refine your selections while building your websites and applications. These filters can be applied directly to your selectors. For example, you may want to select a **div** containing some particular text. You'd write your selector like this:

`$('div:contains("my text")')`

Any **div** containing the text **"my text"** would be selected, allowing you to apply any of the jQuery methods to it.

For filter extensions exclusive to jQuery you'll want to use the **filter()** method to gain back lost performance. (**Table 1.2** shows all the jQuery filter extensions.) The jQuery filter extensions are not part of the current CSS specification; therefore the native DOM methods, specifically **querySelectorAll()**, are not aware of the jQuery extensions. This will cause the jQuery library and the browser's JavaScript engine to carry the greater overhead when processing jQuery's nonstandard extensions. For each of the extensions used, a bit of performance can be lost and, over time, can add up to make your application sluggish. A good example is when you're selecting elements where an attribute is

TABLE 1.2 jQuery Filter Extensions

Filter Name	What It Selects
:animated	All elements being animated at the time the selector is run.
[name!="value"]	Elements either not having the specified attribute, or having the specified attribute but not with a specific value.
:eq()	The element at the specified index within the matched set, zero-based index.
:even	Even elements in a group, zero-based index.
:first	The first matched element.
:gt()	All elements having an index greater than the index within the matched set, zero-based index.
:has()	Elements that contain at least one element matching the specified selector. The selector can be any jQuery selector or combination of selectors.
:header	All header elements: **h1**, **h2**, **h3**, etc.
:hidden	All hidden elements, such as a form element having the **type="hidden"** attribute.
:last	The last matched element in a set of elements.
:lt()	All elements having an index less than the index within the matched set, zero-based index.
:odd	Odd elements in a group, zero-based index.
:parent	All elements that are the parent of another element, including text nodes.
:selected	All elements selected in a form select list.
:visible	All visible elements.

not equal to a certain value, written like this:

```
$('input[name!="myName"]')
```

To gain back the lost performance, apply the **filter()** method to the selector:

```
$('input').filter('[name!="myName"]')
```

You can use the **.filter()** method with all of the filter selectors, but you won't notice any performance gain when you use it with those selectors currently in the CSS specification. Those filters are often known as CSS pseudo-classes. (CSS pseudo-classes are listed in **Table 1.3**.)

Let's take a look at how to use the basic filters first.

TIP You'll find jQuery extensions in all of the filter groups, so to make coding easier you may want to use the **filter()** method any time you use one of the filter selectors. That way you don't have to keep track of which filter is an extension and which isn't.

TIP Older versions of jQuery lower than version 1.7 have other filter extensions available, most notably for forms. Those additional extensions can be found online at http://api.jquery.com/category/selectors/jquery-selector-extensions/.

TABLE 1.3 CSS Pseudo-Class Selectors

Filter Name	What It Selects
:link	All unvisited links.
:visited	All visited links.
:active	The active link.
:hover	Links on mouseover.
:focus	The input element that has focus.
:first-letter	The first letter of every matched element.
:first-line	The first line of every matched element.
:first-child	Every element that is the first child of its parent.
:before	Insert content before the content of every selected element.
:after	Insert content after every selected element.
:only-child	Every matched element that is the only child of its parent.
:nth-child(n)	Every matched element that is the *nth* child of its parent.
:nth-last-child(n)	Every matched element that is the *nth* child of its parent, counting from the last child.
:last-child	Every matched element that is the last child of its parent.
:root	The document's root element.
:empty	Every element that has no children (including text nodes).
:enabled	Every enabled element.
:disabled	Every disabled element.
:checked	Every checked element.
:not(selector)	Every element that is not a **this** element.

To use the basic filters:

1. Open the basic HTML template and add the following markup to the body of the template (you can also follow along in Script **1.3.html**):

```
<ul>
    <li id="first">First Item</li>
    <li id="second">Second
     Item</li>
    <li id="third">Third Item</li>
    <li id="fourth">Fourth Item</li>
</ul>
```

2. Add the following jQuery code to the head of the document (remember to place the jQuery code between `<script></script>` tags):

```
$(document).ready(function() {
$('li:not(#third)').css({'border
 :'1px solid #0000FF'});
});
```

3. Save the file as **basic_filter.html** and load into your browser. The first, second, and fourth list items will have a border around them, but the third will not **Ⓐ**.

> **TIP** If you use the :not filter often, you can make your code more readable and easier to maintain by using the .not() method.

> **TIP** Because HTML5 is being used in the examples, you are no longer required to add the declaration type="text/javascript" to the <script> tag.

Ⓐ The CSS has not been applied to the element you filtered with the **:not()** selector.

- First Item
- Second Item
- Third Item
- Fourth Item

B The third list item is highlighted because it contains the word **"Third"**.

To use the content filters:

1. Make the following modification, adding CSS to the head section of the **basic_ filter.html** (see Script **1.4.html** in the sample code.):

```
<!-- CSS -->
<style>
.highlight {
    background-color: #FFFF00;
}
</style>
```

2. Place this line of jQuery code within your document-ready wrapper:

```
$('li:contains("Third")')
.addClass('highlight');
```

3. Save the updated file as **content_ filter.html**. The result, when loaded into a web browser, is that any list item containing the word **"Third"** will get a background color based on the CSS class highlight **B**.

Any list item containing the word **"Third"** will be selected. Keep in mind that you're not limited to one word in your string, and the **:contains()** filter can only be used on text. The letter case matters, so be sure to double-check your code if you're not finding the match you're after.

The **add_class()** method is a function used to manipulate DOM elements by allowing you to add complex classes to those elements easily. You'll learn more about **addClass()** in Chapter 3, "Getting and Setting DOM Attributes."

TIP HTML5 allows you to use the <style> tag without adding the type="text/css" declaration.

TIP Content filters are case sensitive. "Third" will not match "third".

To use the filter extensions:

1. Using the web page you created (**content_filter.html**), add the following line of jQuery to code you created earlier (Script **1.5.html**):

    ```
    $('li').filter(':first')
    .css({'color':'#FF0000'});
    ```

2. Save the updated file as **extended_filter.html** on your web server and load the file into a web browser. The first list item is now red **C**.

You can use selector filtering to apply jQuery's methods to specific elements or groups of elements not as easily defined, such as portions of a list or certain rows in a table.

Fortunately, the jQuery library provides several selector filters and combinations to track down elements when the need arises. For instance, the **:gt** and **:lt** filters can grab a portion of a group of elements starting at a specific point in the group.

```
$('li').filter(':lt(3)').addClass
  ('highlight');
```

This line of jQuery would apply the **highlight** class to the first three list elements in an unordered list. Selectors like this create a zero-based index on the elements, which means you start counting elements from 0.

```
<ul>
    <li>Index 0</li>
    <li>Index 1</li>
    <li>Index 2</li>
    <li>Index 3</li>
    <li>Index 4</li>
</ul>
```

The class would be applied to the items with index 0, 1, and 2.

C The power of the basic selectors and filters start to become evident when applying styles with pinpoint accuracy.

TIP jQuery also provides a traversal method, `slice()`, which provides very fine-grained ability to select groups of items. You'll learn more about `slice()` in Chapter 6.

Row 1 - Index 0
Row 2 - Index 1
Row 3 - Index 2
Row 4 - Index 3
Row 5 - Index 4
Row 6 - Index 5
Row 7 - Index 6
Row 8 - Index 7
Row 9 - Index 8
Row 10 - Index 9

D The odd rows in the table have been highlighted.

To use the :even or :odd filters:

1. Open the basic HTML template in your text editor and add the following CSS to the head of the document (Script **1.6.html**):

   ```
   <style>
   .highlight { background-color:
   → #FFFF00;}
   td { border: 1px solid #333333;
   → padding: 2px;}
   </style>
   ```

2. Add this markup to the body of the template to create a table:

   ```
   <table>
   <tr><td>Row 1 - Index 0</td></tr>
   <tr><td>Row 2 - Index 1</td></tr>
   <tr><td>Row 3 - Index 2</td></tr>
   <tr><td>Row 4 - Index 3</td></tr>
   <tr><td>Row 5 - Index 4</td></tr>
   <tr><td>Row 6 - Index 5</td></tr>
   <tr><td>Row 7 - Index 6</td></tr>
   <tr><td>Row 8 - Index 7</td></tr>
   <tr><td>Row 9 - Index 8</td></tr>
   <tr><td>Row 10 - Index 9</td></tr>
   </table>
   ```

3. Place the jQuery code in the head of the document. Don't forget to place it within the document-ready function:

   ```
   $('tr').filter(':odd')
   .addClass('highlight');
   ```

4. Save the file as **odd.html** and load it into your web browser. You'll see that every other row of the table has the highlight class applied to it **D**.

Index numbers were included in the table to demonstrate that the **:odd** selector is one of the filters using zero-based indexes. If you change the filter to **:even**, the first row and every even indexed row will be selected.

TIP jQuery's **:nth-child()** filter uses a one-based index, so you'd start counting the selected elements from 1. The **:nth-child** filter is not an extension; rather, it's a part of the **CSS** specification.

Some of the most useful selectors are the attribute selectors. You can use them by themselves or in combination with one of the basic selectors to create jQuery objects from elements you've already included in your HTML markup. Here's an example:

```
$('img[src="foo.jpg"]').css({
→ 'border':'2px solid #0000FF' });
```

Here you've applied a style property to a picture, **foo.jpg**, within your web page. Being able to select the element without having to add a class or an ID allows you to create your HTML markup without worrying about how you'll use jQuery to enhance your website later **E**.

E Here is a really cool picture from the 1970s with a blue border added to it via the **css()** method.

To use an attribute selector:

1. Put the following CSS into the head of your boilerplate HTML file (Script **1.7.html**):

```
.alert {
    background-color: #FFFF00;
    color: #FF0000;
}
```

2. Create a small form in the body:

```
<form action="" method="post">
<input name="firstName"
→ placeholder="First Name" />
<span class="alert"></span><br />
<input name="lastName"
→ placeholder="Last Name" />
→ <span class="alert"></span><br />
<input name="emailAddress"
→ placeholder="E-Mail Address"/>
<span class="alert"></span><br />
<input type="submit" value="Send
→ Your Info" />
</form>
```

3. Add the jQuery function designed to check the length of the value of the e-mail field:

```
$('input[name="emailAddress"]')
.blur(function(){
if(0 == $(this).val().length) {
$(this).next('.alert').text(
→ 'Please fill in your e-mail
→ address');
} else {
$(this).next('.alert').text('');
}
});
```

4. Save the file using the name **attribute.html**. Place the file on your web server and load the page into your web browser Ⓖ.

5. Tab through each field without filling out any information. When you tab or click away from the e-mail field, the alert message will appear Ⓗ.

6. Type some characters into the e-mail field, and then tab or click away from the field, and the alert message will disappear.

In this exercise you used a number of methods: **blur()**, a form event; **next()**, a DOM traversal method; **text()**, a DOM manipulation method; **val()**, a method you can use to get and set attribute values; and **length**, a JavaScript measurement function.

When you tab or click away from a field, a blur event occurs. Creating a function to be triggered by an event (a common task when using jQuery) is easy to do. The function you created here looks at the length of the value of the form field to see if it's zero. If the length value is zero, the function looks for the next element having the alert class and then changes the text of the element. More details about these functions will be discussed later in this book.

There are a number of versions of the attribute selectors. You can select the beginning or end of an attribute value, a substring of the value, or even whether the element has a particular attribute. You'll learn a lot more about the attribute selectors in Chapter 5, "Harnessing Advanced Selectors."

| First Name |
| Last Name |
| E-Mail Address |
| Send Your Info |

Ⓖ Here is your simple form.

| First Name |
| Last Name |
| | Please fill in your e-mail address |
| Send Your Info |

Ⓗ Be sure to fill in the e-mail field!

Rewind and Review

Take a few moments to reflect on what you've learned in this chapter:

- What are the four basic jQuery selector types?

- How can you combine selectors to allow you to apply jQuery methods and functions to more than one set of elements?

- Why should you apply the **filter()** method with jQuery's filter extensions?

- When referring to a set of selected elements, what is a zero-based index?

- If you change the jQuery selector in the example for **$(this)** from **$('#secondLink')** to **$('a')**, what do you think will happen?

- Can using an attribute selector prevent you from having to use IDs and classes?

What Is $(this)?

Many developers new to JavaScript and other object-oriented languages often have a hard time coming to grips with **$(this)** because JavaScript also has an object named **this**. Since jQuery *is* JavaScript, what's the difference?

When used alone, **this** is a JavaScript object on which the current JavaScript method is acting. In other words, **this** will be seen in JavaScript functions. You can apply JavaScript methods to **this**, but you cannot apply jQuery methods to the object because **this** is not in scope for jQuery functions.

In jQuery **$(this)** is an object, usually the items contained in a selector. The object has immediate access to all of the jQuery methods. You will see the **$(this)** object used within jQuery functions.

The **$(this)** object (or any selected element) in jQuery also has access to the JavaScript methods and functions due to jQuery's relationship with JavaScript. Being able to use jQuery's **$(this)** object gives you tremendous flexibility when you're designing functions to make your websites and applications more powerful and interactive.

Have a look at Script **1.8.html** by opening it in your text editor and loading it into your browser for an example of how **this** and **$(this)** work. In the pure JavaScript example, **this** (referring to the link) is passed to the function **clicked()** using an inline JavaScript call.

In the jQuery function, a selector is used to identify the clicked link and the **$(this)** object is used within the **click()** function.

Both functions then use the JavaScript **length** function to get the number of characters in the link's text.

When either link is clicked, the number of characters in the link text is displayed in the browser using an **alert()** function **F**.

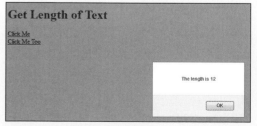

F The alert is fired for the second link on the page.

2

Handling Events

The single most common task you'll find yourself performing with jQuery is event handling. Browser events, mouse events, and keyboard events are easily directed and interpreted by the jQuery library's methods and functions.

When you combine the event-handling capability of jQuery with the ability to easily select DOM elements, you get a powerful and easy-to-use combination. For instance, a single mouse click can set off a chain of instructions, such as including animations, sending information to a server, or changing the text of the page. A blur event (as seen in Chapter 1, "Using Selectors") can be used to trigger functions to check the value in a form field or trigger an Ajax request. You can capture when the mouse cursor hovers over elements in the page to create image rollovers or reveal more information to your website visitors.

In this chapter, you'll explore event handlers and learn how to attach and use them with jQuery selectors to create unique interactions and trigger other processes.

In This Chapter

Attaching Event Handlers

With the advent of jQuery 1.7, attaching event handlers to selectors was made easier and more readable by focusing on event methods directly. In the days before the newer versions of jQuery, it was not uncommon to see the following syntax to attach a click event handler to a selector:

```
$('element').bind('click', function() {
...});
```

jQuery has added many shortcut methods to simplify your coding, so now you can write the following syntax to accomplish the same thing:

```
$('element').click(function() {...});
```

Under the hood, jQuery handles the binding of the event handler without all of the additional code.

You'll typically be attaching to four common events categorized as browser events, form events, keyboard events, and mouse events.

In addition, there are some more specialized event handlers. You've already used one of them, the `ready()` event handler. The `ready()` event handler executes when the DOM has been completely loaded into the browser. Typically, this event handler is used to prevent your jQuery code from running until all of the elements are in place for your jQuery code to select.

Building a Website

The most practical way to learn how to use jQuery is by including it in a website. Starting with this chapter, you'll build a website from the ground up based on the markup and code scripts included in Appendix B, "An Active jQuery Website."

In Appendix B, all the code is set out for you and is available in the downloadable code examples package. You'll be taking portions of the example code during each exercise and applying jQuery to the markup. Additionally, the code for each exercise will be supplied separately as you grow the site.

You'll also be using some basic code organization principles, as the HTML5, CSS3, and jQuery files will be separate from each other and stored in subdirectories where needed. All of the jQuery files will be stored in the `inc/` folder, under the root of the markup file.

Although you will gain insight into HTML5 and CSS3, this book doesn't go into detail about how to use those technologies. For more insight into HTML5 and CSS3, read:

Introducing HTML5 (Peachpit Press) by Bruce Lawson and Remy Sharp

Practical CSS3: Develop and Design (Peachpit Press) by Chris Mills

HTML5 and CSS3 Visual QuickStart Guide (Peachpit Press) by Elizabeth Castro and Bruce Hyslop

Calling Document Events

Because jQuery typically interacts with elements in your web pages, you'll want to make sure all of the elements are loaded into the browser before any of the jQuery methods are called. To accomplish this, you'd use the **ready()** event handler to make sure all of the DOM elements are loaded. There are a couple of ways to capture the event, and you can use either one of these methods—directly in your page's markup or in a separate file.

To use the ready() handler in a separate file:

1. Open a blank document in your text editor and attach the **ready()** handler to the document:

   ```
   $(document).ready(function() {
       // your jQuery code goes here
   });
   ```

   Or you can use

   ```
   $(function() {
       // your jQuery code goes here
   });
   ```

2. Save the file with the name **jquery.custom.js** in the **inc/jquery/** folder for use in the website you'll be building.

3. In your HTML files, place the following line in the head section after the line you set to call the jQuery core library:

   ```
   <script src="inc/jquery/jquery.
   ↪ custom.js"></script>
   ```

   If you're only going to use one or two jQuery methods in a web page, you may opt to just write all of your jQuery code within the web page itself.

To use the ready() handler in a web page:

1. Create an HTML file in your text editor or load one of the boilerplate templates provided in Appendix B.

2. Attach the **ready()** handler to the document by adding the following markup and code within the head tags after the line where you've included the jQuery core library:

```
<script>
$(document).ready(function() {
    // your jQuery code goes here
});
</script>
```

Or you can use

```
<script>
$(function() {
    // your jQuery code goes here
});
</script>
```

The **$(function() {...});** syntax is a shorthand method for calling the **ready()** event handler.

Keep in mind you don't have to include your jQuery within the head tags at the top of the page. You can add script tags anywhere in the page; you'll often see other developers place their jQuery code within script tags at the bottom of the page. They can be assured all of the DOM elements have loaded by the time the jQuery code is parsed when they include it at the bottom of a page. It's a matter of personal preference and code organization.

TIP The document may be fully loaded into the browser, but that doesn't mean the page has completely loaded. The **ready()** event handler only accounts for all of the DOM elements. Images and other media may still be loading when the handler has signaled that the DOM is ready to go.

TIP If your jQuery code isn't working, check first to make sure the code is wrapped in the ready handler or the shorthand function.

TIP The name for the JavaScript file is not important as long as you remember to include it properly. Including *jquery* in the name helps with organization and maintenance.

Now that you've checked to make sure the document is loaded, it's time to start handling other events in your web pages. Let's begin with the shortcuts for mouse events.

Trapping Mouse Events

Though it may seem simple, the mouse is actually one of the most efficient and versatile tools available to computer users. The mouse makes it easy to navigate websites and select information you wish to see or interact with. For many, the mouse is the most used piece of hardware (from a physical contact standpoint) attached to a computer.

The reason is simple—the mouse is easy to comprehend and is user-friendly. Because people use the mouse extensively, jQuery has provided a number of event handlers for the mouse (see **Table 2.1**) that you can take advantage of. The most basic of these is the click event.

TABLE 2.1 The jQuery Mouse Events

Handler Name	Handler Usage
click()	Handles the click event, or trigger the event on an element.
dblclick()	Use with the dblclick event, or to trigger the event on an element.
focusin()	Use to handle the instant when an element receives focus; can also be fired with the keyboard.
focusout()	Handles the instant that the element loses focus with either the mouse or the keyboard.
hover()	Binds two handlers to the selected elements, one to be executed when the mouse pointer enters the elements, and one to be triggered when the mouse pointer leaves the elements.
mousedown()	An event handler called when a mouse button is activated.
mouseup()	An event handler called when a mouse button is released.
mouseenter()	Causes an event handler to be fired when the mouse enters an element.
mouseleave()	An event handler fired when the mouse leaves an element.
mousemove()	Handles the event caused by mouse movement when the event is bound to an element. Can be used to track mouse position within an element.
mouseover()	Use to handle the event triggered by moving the mouse cursor into an area.
mouseout()	Use to handle the event caused by moving the mouse away from an area.

To use the click event handler:

1. Using the HTML boilerplate template (**html5_boilerplate.html** in Appendix B), add the following markup to create a form in a **div** with an **id="registration"**. Save the file as **index.html** (Script **2.1.html**).

```
<div id="registration">
<form action="inc/php/
→ registration.php"
→ method="post">
<input type="text" name=
→ "userEMail" placeholder="your
→ e-mailaddress"
/>
<button type="submit">Subscribe
→ </button>
</form>
<a href="">Click Here to
→ Subscribe</a>
</div>
```

2. Copy the style sheet folder and **base.css** style sheet to a directory below your **index.html** file (Script **css/base.css**). Your directory structure should look like **Ⓐ**.

3. Upload the **index.html** file and the CSS folder along with **base.css** to your web server and open **index.html** in your web browser. If everything is in place, your page will look like **Ⓑ**. Clicking on the link should not cause anything to happen.

4. Create the **inc/jquery/** directory to hold the jQuery files below your **index.html** file as seen in **Ⓐ**.

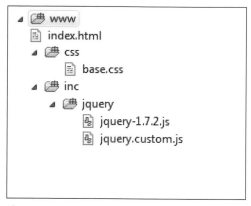

Ⓐ This is the directory structure you'll use to build the website.

Ⓑ The link element for the form is visible, but the form is hidden off the top of the page.

C The animation triggered by the click event reveals the registration form.

5. Open the **jquery.custom.js** in your text editor and add the following code (Script **inc/jquery/jquery.custom.js**):

```
$('#registration a')
.click(function(event){
event.preventDefault();
if(false ==8 $('#registration')
.hasClass('open')) {
$('#registration').animate({
    'top': '0px'
}, 500, function(){
$('#registration')
.addClass('open');
});
} else {
$('#registration').animate({
    'top': '-40px'
}, 500, function(){
$('#registration')
.removeClass('open');
});
}
});
```

6. Save the file as **jquery.custom.js** in the **inc/jquery/** directory and be sure to upload the directory with the file to your web server.

7. Reload **index.html** in your browser and try clicking on the link. The registration form should animate downward after the first click **C**.

Clicking the link again should make the registration **div** move upward to hide the form.

continues on next page

Did everything work as you expected it to? Were any errors generated? If you had errors, you'll want to look for error messages, such as those generated by Firebug 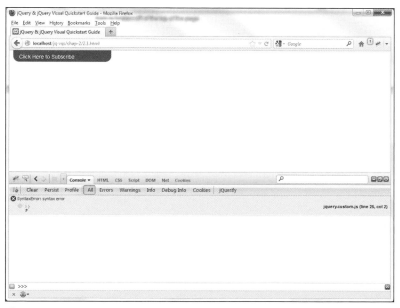.

In this exercise you used a number of jQuery methods: **preventDefault()**, part of the JavaScript event object; **hasClass()**, which allows you to get CSS class information from an element (see Chapter 3, "Getting and Setting DOM Attributes"); **animate()**, a custom method used to perform animations on CSS properties (Chapter 8, "Creating Captivating Effects"); **addClass()**, which sets any number of CSS classes on a jQuery object (Chapter 3); and **removeClass()**, which removes classes from a jQuery object (also in Chapter 3).

TIP Documenting your code is always a good idea. Place as many comments in your code as you find necessary. This will make the code easier to maintain and fix should something go haywire.

When you click on the link, a click event is generated. In this example you use the click event to either open or close the sliding drawer based on whether the drawer has the class **open**. The default behavior of the link, which is normally to navigate to another page, is bypassed so that the animation can be performed.

Let's apply the animation concept for the basic page navigation but using jQuery's **hover()** method. The **hover()** method is actually two functions in one: a function for the mouseenter event with another function for the mouseleave event.

D Oops! The error is displayed in Firebug.

To use the hover() method:

1. Edit and then save the **index.html** file you created in the first exercise, adding the following markup for the website navigation (Script **2.2.html**):

```
<div id="navigation">
<a href="content_index.html">
→ Home</a>
<a href="content_product.html">
→ Products</a>
<a href="content_services.html">
→ Services</a>
<a href="content_about.html">
→ About Us</a><br />
<span id="drawer_title">
→ Site Navigation</span>
</div>
```

2. Open **jQuery.custom.js** in your text editor and add the following code within the document ready handler:

```
$('#navigation').hover(function(){
$(this).stop().animate({
    'top': '0px'
});
},function(){
$(this).stop().animate({
    'top': '-40px'
});
});
```

3. Save both files to your web server and load **index.html** into your web browser. Move your mouse cursor over the Site Navigation drawer. The drawer should move down to reveal the site navigation links  (E).

Because the animation is triggered by the mouse's position, there's no need to add a class to the drawer as you did in the click exercise. In this example you did use another jQuery method, **stop()**, which is another of the custom animation methods. You'll learn more about the **stop()** method in Chapter 8.

> **TIP** The hover() and toggle() methods are the only jQuery methods made up of two functions.

continues on next page

E The navigation drawer is opened to show the navigation elements.

There are some subtle differences in some of the mouse events. The **hover()** method you used in the exercise captures the mouseenter event during the first function and the mouseleave event for the second function. If you wanted to change the event handlers to the **mouseover()** and **mouseout()** methods, you'd end up writing two selectors and binding them to the individual events, but the result would be the same.

```
$('#navigation').
→ mouseover(function(){
    $(this).stop().animate({
        'top': '0px'
    });
});
$('#navigation').
→ mouseout(function(){
    $(this).stop().animate({
        'top': '-40px'
    });
});
```

As you continue to build the website, you'll use some of the other mouse event handlers, and their specialized use will be explained more fully.

The second most common way to interact with a web page is using the keyboard. Let's have a look at the event handlers for the keyboard next.

TABLE 2.2 jQuery Keyboard Events

Event Name	Handler Usage
focusin()	Use this to determine when a focusin event has occurred; can also be used as a mouse event.
focusout()	Use this to determine when a focusout event has occurred; can also be used as a mouse event.
keydown()	Use this to capture the keydown event.
keypress()	Use this to capture the keypress event; may be browser specific.
keyup()	Use this to capture the keyup event.

Capturing Keyboard Events

You'll find that capturing and using keyboard events is a common task as you build a jQuery-enabled website. These events fall into two distinct categories: capturing when a key has been pressed or released, and determining which key was pressed. For now let's focus on the event handlers shown in **Table 2.2**, which determine when a key has been pressed or released.

To use the keyup() event handler:

1. Edit the `comments.html` file in your text editor and add the following markup for a comments form (Script **2.3.html**):

```
<div id="content">

<p>Send us your comments, we'd
→ love to hear from you!</p>

<p class="textInfo">You have typed
→ <span>0</span> characters.</p>

<form name="contact" action="inc/
→ php/contact.php" method="post">

<input type="text" name=
→ "contactName"

placeholder="your name"/><br />

<input type="text" name=
→ "contactEMail"

placeholder= "your e-mail
→ address"/><br />

<textarea name="contactComments"
→ placeholder="your comments">
→ </textarea><br />
```

continues on next page

```
<button type="submit" name=
→"submit">Send your comments
→</button>

</form>

</div>
```

2. Open **jquery.custom.js** to add the following code to count the characters entered into the form's **textarea**:

```
$('textarea[name=
→"contactComments"]')

.keyup(function(){

var numCharacters =

$(this).val().length;

$('.textInfo span')

.html(numCharacters);

});
```

You have typed 17 characters.

your name

your e-mail address

I have an opinion

Send your comments

A The count of characters is updated with each keystroke.

3. Save and upload both files to their appropriate directories on your web server and load the **comments.html** page into your web browser. Start typing in the **textarea** and you'll see that the span in the following markup is updated with the count of the keystrokes entered into the **textarea** **A**.

```
<p class="textInfo">You have typed
<span>0</span> characters.</p>
```

You've bound the **keyup()** event handler to the **textarea** using an attribute selector (more on those in Chapter 5, "Harnessing Advanced Selectors"). When a keyup event occurs within the **textarea**, the value of the length (or number) of characters is determined and placed into the variable **numCharacters**. The variable is then used to modify the HTML of the span within the **textInfo** class. The **html()** method is a DOM insertion method you'll learn more about in Chapter 4, "Manipulating DOM Elements."

You have typed 2 characters.

```
your name
your e-mail address
Two
```

Send your comments

B Something is not quite right when counting with the **keydown()** event handler.

Is it important to know whether the keyup or keydown event occurred while typing in the text box? For the purposes of this exercise, knowing which event occurred—and, more importantly, when the event occurs—is the key to making the character counter work properly. If you change to the **keydown()** event handler, you'll see that typing the first character doesn't change the counter. The keydown event is fired before the value in the text box is changed. The counter isn't changed until the second character is typed (keydown) and will be one less than you expect it to be because the second keydown event has occurred before the value is updated again **B**.

Using the **keyup()** event handler is the proper way to count the characters because the text box is updated during the keydown event and the counting function is triggered when the keyup event occurs.

TIP The JavaScript keypress event is browser specific and in some cases specific to certain browser versions. jQuery uses normalization for these kinds of events behind the scenes and makes the event handler work cross-browser. In most cases, you'll only need to use the keyup() or the keydown() event handler.

TIP It's important to know when events are triggered. You should always consider this when choosing your event handlers.

Let's use a keyboard event handler with a counting function for a different purpose—making sure a form field hasn't been left blank.

To use the focusout() method:

1. Modify the form in the **comments.html** file by adding an empty span element to the end of the contact name and contact e-mail fields (Script **2.4.html**):

```
<input type="text"
name="contactName"
placeholder="your name"/>
<span></span><br />
<input type="text"
name="contactEMail"
placeholder= "your e-mail
→ address"/>
<span></span><br />
```

2. Add the following block of code to your custom jQuery file:

```
$('input[name="contactName"]')
.focusout(function(){
if(0 == $(this).val().length) {
    $(this).next('span')
    .html(' please do not
    → leave name blank')
    .css({'color': '#FF0000'});
} else {
    $(this).next('span').html('');
}
});
```

3. Upload both files to the web server and reload the **comments.html** file in your web browser. Place the cursor into the name field and then tab to the next field without placing any text into the input. The error message will appear .

C A friendly reminder to fill out the name field.

In this exercise, you attached the **focusout()** event handler to the contact name field of the form. When the field has the focus (when you place the cursor within it) and then loses the focus based on a keyboard event (a tab in the example) or a mouse event (clicking something else on the page), the **focusout()** event handler triggers a series of methods to create and display or remove an error message in the span tag you added to the markup in Step 1.

Along the way you used the **next()** function, which is a tree traversal method, and the **html()** function, which is a DOM manipulation method.

TIP The focusin and focusout events are not limited to form elements. Many browsers are capable of registering these two events on every element in a web page.

TIP Checking to make sure the field is not blank is a very basic method of performing form validation. Using jQuery, you can only validate the form on the client side. Even when performing client-side validation, you should always perform server-side validation. Always. Performing both client-side and server-side validation is insurance to make sure no one is trying to break your server with things like SQL injection or cross-site hacking attacks.

You're becoming an event-handling pro! But there's one category of event handlers we haven't covered yet: events specific to forms. That's up next!

Forging Form Events

Early on in the development of jQuery it was noticed that form elements are somewhat unique in web pages. As opposed to static text or images, the form is something a website visitor actually interacts with in more than rudimentary ways. Filling out, selecting, checking, and choosing provide interactions that allow the user to send something to the website owner or get more information from the website's database.

Because the interaction provided with forms is unique, the jQuery library provides five powerful event handlers specifically designed to be used with forms (see **Table 2.3**). In the following exercise, you'll modify the form you created earlier and attach various event handlers to enhance the interaction with the form elements.

Let's start with the **blur()** event handler to trigger validation of the e-mail address.

TABLE 2.3 The jQuery Form Event Handlers

Handler Name	Handler Usage
blur()	Use this event handler for triggering functions when an input loses focus.
change()	Use this event handler when a change event is triggered by re-entering text in an input or by selecting something new from a drop-down list.
focus()	Use this event handler to trigger functions when an element gains focus.
select()	Use this event handler when performing the select event, such as selecting text.
submit()	Use this event handler to trigger functions upon a form submission.

To use the blur() event handler:

1. Open the **jquery.custom.js** file and place the following code within the document ready handler:

```
$('input[name="contactEMail"]')
.blur(function() {
var regexEmail = /^[a-zA-Z0-9._-
    ]+@[a-zA-Z0-9.-]+\.[a-zA-Z]{2,4}$/;
var inputEmail = $(this).val();
var resultEmail = regexEmail.
    test(inputEmail);
if(!resultEmail){
    $(this).next('span').html(' 
        please enter a valid e-mail
        address').css({
        'color': '#FF0000'
    });
    } else {
        $(this).next('span').
            html('');
    }
});
```

No changes have to be made to **comments.html** (Script **2.4.html**) because you added the span tags to the form in a previous exercise.

2. Save the jQuery file and upload it to the proper place on your server.

3. Reload the **comments.html** file into your browser and place the cursor within the e-mail input. Then tab or click away from the input. The error message should appear because the field is blank **Ⓐ**.

4. Go back to the field and type a nonstandard e-mail address, such as **jquery@**. Tab or click away from the input and the error message should remain.

5. Type a valid e-mail address into the field, then tab or click away. The error message should disappear.

There are some items in this function that you've never seen before, most notably the expression contained in the **regexEmail** variable and the JavaScript **test()** method.

The expression contained in the **regexEmail** is known as a *regular expression*. Essentially a regular expression is a pattern you can use to test the formation of a text string. Learning and using regular expressions provides you with a tool for testing complex strings of information like an e-mail address.

continues on next page

You have typed 0 characters.

your name

your e-mail address   please enter a valid e-mail address

Send your comments

Ⓐ The error message generated when the e-mail field is not valid.

When the blur event occurs, the value of the form field is placed into a variable (`inputEmail`).

The JavaScript `test()` method breaks down like this: take the regular expression and test it on the value of the input field. If there's a match, the function returns "true". If there's no match, the function returns "false". In the exercise you set the value of `resultEmail` to the value the function returned.

```
var resultEmail = regexEmail.
→ test(inputEmail);
```

Once the value of the variable is set, you can test it in the `if` conditional:

```
if(!resultEmail) {...}
```

Reading this condition out loud, you would say, "if not true `resultEmail`". Sure, reading it out loud makes you sound as if you were a wise old character from a science fiction movie, but it makes sense. The exclamation point before the variable is the "not" condition. Remove the exclamation point to test for a "true" condition.

TIP The `blur()` method is slightly different from the `focusout()` event handler because `focusout()` can detect when a parent element loses focus.

TIP Regardless of how much client-side validation you perform, you should always perform server-side validation.

The `blur()` event handler is also used by the `change()` event handler when information is changed within an input or text area. But the `change()` event handler has an added bonus: it can also check when a change has occurred due to a mouse selection in a select list. Ready to see this in action?

More on Regular Expressions

Regular expressions are patterns that can be parsed by a regular expression engine, such as the engine provided by JavaScript. These patterns can be used to test strings to make sure there is a match between the string and the regular expression pattern.

A full discussion of regular expressions goes beyond the scope of this book, but you can learn more about regular expressions and even test those expressions by visiting the following websites:

www.regular-expressions.info/ is a comprehensive site on the subject, with many clear examples.

http://regexlib.com/ is a searchable library of some of the most commonly used regular expressions.

www.visibone.com/regular-expressions/ is a regular-expression quick reference.

http://regexpal.com/ is an online regular-expression tester.

You don't have to be an expert in regular expressions in order to use jQuery, but using them can supercharge your code when it's necessary to match complex information strings.

You have typed 0 characters.

your name

your e-mail address

your comments

non-subscriber ▾ your subscriber status has changed

Send your comments

B The status message is shown when the change occurs.

To use the change() event handler:

1. Modify **comments.html** to add a drop-down list below the text area:

```
<select name="subscriberStatus">
    <option></option>
    <option value=
    ⇥"non-subscriber">
    non-subscriber</option>
    <option value="subscriber">
    subscriber</option>
</select><span></span><br />
```

2. Add the following block of code to the **jquery.custom.js** file to attach the change event handler to the selector for the drop-down list:

```
$('select
[name="subscriberStatus"]')
.change(function(){
$(this).next('span')
.html(' your subscriber
⇥status has changed');
});
```

3. Save **comments.html** and place it on your web server. Select a status from the drop-down and the change event will be captured by the event handler to show the message **B**.

As used here, the **change()** event handler provides you with a way to determine when a change is made to a drop-down list. But you can also capture the event when a user makes a change in a text box or input field.

You'll use other event handlers as you continue to build the website.

TIP The change() event handler can also be used on drop-down boxes where multiple selections are allowed.

Rewind and Review

You were introduced to a lot of new concepts in this chapter. Take a moment to reflect on what you've learned.

- What are the four basic event-handler types?

- Which event handler is used to determine when the DOM has completed loading?

- Are you limited on the number of functions you can trigger with an event handler?

- How many functions are there in the **hover()** method?

- Why is the order in which an event occurs important?

- Should you do server-side validation when you perform client-side validation?

- What's the difference between the **focusout()** and the **blur()** event handlers?

- What is a regular expression?

- What is the shorthand method for the document ready handler?

Getting and Setting DOM Attributes

Imagine being able to have access to every property and attribute of every element in your web pages. Now imagine you have total control over those properties and attributes. Would having that level of access and control make your web development life easier?

The jQuery library gives you the access and control you desire over each element's attributes and properties. Known collectively as the DOM (Document Object Model) general attribute methods, these powerful functions allow you to get or set attributes and properties, add and remove classes, and even directly set Cascading Style Sheet (CSS) properties on elements or groups of elements, as seen in Chapter 1, "Using Selectors."

In this chapter, you'll learn what the difference is between properties and attributes in your markup and how to use jQuery's functions (see **Table 3.1** on the next page) to get and set them. You'll also gain insight into some of the ways different browsers treat properties and attributes. On with the show!

TABLE 3.1 jQuery Attribute Methods

Function Name	Use It To...
attr()	Get the value of an attribute for the first element in the set of matched elements.
removeAttr()	Remove an attribute from each element in the set of matched elements.
prop()	Add or set a property or get the value of a property.
removeProp()	Remove a property for the set of matched elements.
val()	Use with form elements to get or set the current value of the first element in the set of matched elements.
addClass()	Add the specified class or classes to each of the set of matched elements.
hasClass()	Test whether any of the matched elements are assigned the given class.
removeClass()	Remove a class or classes from each element in the set of matched elements.
toggleClass()	Add or remove one or more classes from each element in the set of matched elements, depending on whether the class is already present or not present on the element.

Understanding the DOM

The Document Object Model (DOM) is an applications programming interface (API) that gives languages like JavaScript access to the inner workings of web pages. This allows you, the web developer, a way to make changes to the content, the style, and even the structure of your web page documents.

When a web page is requested from a server, the bits and pieces making up the document are sent to the browser. When those pieces arrive at the browser, they're assembled and parsed according to how the browser creator interprets the document model (a discussion much too long, and heated, for this book). The browser then renders the document.

One of the key things you need to understand is that all of the markup, the DOM, is loaded first, and then other media such as graphics, pictures, video, and audio. The DOM can be ready to go well before the page finishes loading and rendering in your browser.

It's also important that you understand the fact that different browsers parse and render the DOM differently—sometimes drastically. Be sure to test your websites in various browsers before making your creations available to the public.

Changing Properties

Before we delve into getting and changing properties on HTML elements, it's important to understand the difference between attributes and properties.

Under normal circumstances, properties are parts of an HTML element and can be set with a Boolean value or the original state of certain elements at the time the DOM is loaded.

But attributes might have one of many values, such as the name attribute on form elements or IDs and classes on any element. The advent of HTML5 gives you custom *data elements*, attributes you can name and use as storage for various bits of information you might use with CSS or jQuery.

The best way to think of properties is that they're like light switches. They're limited to a couple of states (typically Boolean values like true or false). On the other hand, attributes are used to store data and can be quite flexible in their content.

There is one special case where you'll use the property method with an attribute. Let's look at a way to handle the special case first.

Using prop( ) to change an input type:

1. Open **comments.html** in your text editor and add the following markup to your form after the form's e-mail input element (Script **3.1.html**):

```
<input type="text"
→ name="contactPassword"
→ placeholder="password" />

<span></span><br />

<a href="" class="small_text"
→ id="showPassword">Hide Password
→ </a><br />
```

2. Edit **jquery.custom.js** to include the following code:

```
$('#showPassword')

.click(function(e) {

e.preventDefault();

var propertyType = $('input[name="
→ contactPassword"])

.prop('type');

if('text' == propertyType) {

$('input[name="contactPassword"])

.prop('type', 'password');

$(this).html('Show Password');

} else {

$('input[name="contactPassword"])

.prop('type', 'text');

$(this).html('Hide Password');

}

});
```

3. Save both files and upload them to your web server. Load the page into your browser and you should see the addition to the form .

 The new form field for the password.

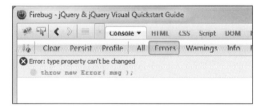

B Visible passwords aren't a good thing, but it may help users when they're creating a lengthy password.

C The old vanishing password trick worked!

D The error message generated in Firebug when you try to use **attr()** to change the type attribute.

4. Type a password into the form and it should be visible to you **B**.

5. Click the Hide Password link and the input's type is changed to **password**, hiding the password **C**.

6. Clicking the Show Password link will reveal the password to the user **B**.

TIP jQuery prohibits changing the type attribute on an **<input>** or **<button>** element using the **attr()** method. Trying to change the type on one of these elements will throw an error in all browsers. This is because older versions of Internet Explorer, prior to version 8, would not allow the change. But by using the jQuery **prop()** method (available since jQuery version 1.6), you can change the attribute **D**.

TIP As it turns out, you can change some attributes with the **prop()** method and some properties with the **attr()** method, but I encourage you to use these methods for their intended purposes. It'll reduce confusion and make your code easier to read, and you'll avoid some inconsistent behaviors from browser to browser.

TIP Custom HTML5 data attributes must begin with **data-**, but you can describe or name the data however you'd like after the hyphen—for instance, **data-author="Jay"** or **data-dessert="pie"**.

In this example you used the **prop()** method in two ways. By using it one way you were able to get the value of the type attribute. The second way allowed you to set the attribute's value. Normally, you'd use the **prop()** method to set Boolean values, such as true or false.

Let's look at the more conventional way to use the **prop()** method.

Using prop() to enable or disable a form element:

1. Edit the password field in **comments.html** (Script **3.2.html**), changing the placeholder and the state of the input:

```
<input type="text"
   name="contactPassword"
   placeholder="password not
   required" DISABLED/>

<span></span><br />
```

2. Add the following code to **jquery.custom.js** to enable or disable the password field as well as change the **placeholder** attribute:

```
$('select[name="subscriberStatus"]')

.change(function() {

var selectValue = $(this).val();

if('subscriber' == selectValue) {

$('input[name="contactPassword"]')

.prop('disabled', false);

$('input[name="contactPassword"]')

.attr('placeholder', 'password
required');

} else {

$('input[name="contactPassword"]')

.prop('disabled', true);

$('input[name="contactPassword"]')

.attr('placeholder', 'password not
   required');

}

});
```

3. Test the function by saving the files to your web server and loading **comments.html** into your browser .

    Try to click into the password field. You'll find that you can't because the field is disabled.

E The password field is not accessible.

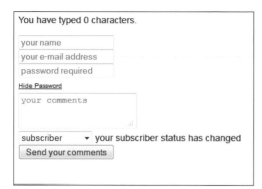

You have typed 0 characters.

your name

your e-mail address

password required

Hide Password

your comments

subscriber ▾ your subscriber status has changed

Send your comments

F The password field is now enabled and the placeholder has changed.

4. Select "subscriber" from the drop-down list. The field is now enabled and the placeholder text is set to "password required" **F**.

In this exercise, you used the `prop()` method to do what it does best: handling Boolean values for elements. You also got a small taste of using the `attr()` function, using it to change the value of the placeholder. As you continue to build the website you'll use `prop()` again, but first let's cover the other property function: `removeProp()`.

To use removeProp():

1. Add the following line of code to `jquery.custom.js`. This code adds a custom property to the password field (no changes are required in `comments.html`):

   ```
   $('input[name="contactPassword"]')
   .prop('defaultStatus',
   → 'non-subscriber');
   ```

2. Insert the following code snippet into `jquery.custom.js` to remove the custom property when the proper change occurs:

   ```
   $('select
   [name="subscriberStatus"]')
   .change(function() {
   var statusValue = $(this).val();
   if('subscriber' == statusValue) {
   $('input [name="contactPassword"]')
   .removeProp('defaultStatus');
   }
   });
   ```

   continues on next page

3. Place the jQuery file on your web server and reload **comments.html**. Looking at a DOM inspector, like Firebug, you can check for the custom property **G**.

4. Select "subscriber" from the drop-down list. Refreshing the DOM inspector will let you see that the property has been removed from the DOM **H**.

Why would you set a custom property? In this exercise, you might want to save the state of the property to the database to determine how many people are using the form without ever choosing to use a password or to track how many users changed the drop-down list.

TIP Never use `removeProp()` to remove native properties like `checked`, `disabled`, or `selected` because these properties will be removed permanently from the current document until a reload or refresh occurs. There is no way to add these properties back into a page once they're removed.

There is one more general attribute function specifically aimed at forms: the `val()` method. Let's take a look at ways to get and set values using the `val()` method.

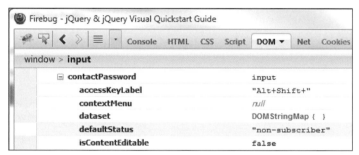

G The custom property `defaultStatus` and its value have been added to the DOM.

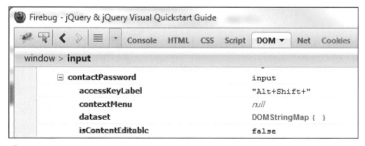

H The custom property is no longer in the DOM.

A The non-subscriber value is selected.

Managing Values

The **val()** method is specifically designed to work with all form elements such as inputs, check boxes, select lists, and text areas. You put it to work for you in Chapter 2, "Handling Events," to get form element values and check those values to make sure they were the proper length or contained the proper information. Using **val()** to get the values from form elements is the most common use of the function.

You can also set values for form elements using the **val()** function. This technique is handy if you want to set a default value or change a value based on the triggering of some other event.

To set the value of an input using val():

1. Add the following line of code to your jQuery file. You don't have to modify **comments.html**:

   ```
   $('select
    [name="subscriberStatus"]')
   .val('non-subscriber');
   ```

2. Place the jQuery file on your web server and load **comments.html** into a browser. The select list should now have the item non-subscriber selected **A**.

To get the value of an input box using val():

1. Add the following function to the **jquery.custom.js** file to test for a strong password (no edits need to be made to **comments.html**):

continues on next page

```
$('input
[name="contactPassword"]')
.blur(function() {
var regexPassword = /(?=^.{8,}$)
→ ((?=.*\d)|(?=.*\W+))(?![.\n])
→ (?=.*[A-Z])(?=.*[a-z]).*$/;
var thisPassword = $(this).val();
var resultPassword =
→ regexPassword.test(thisPassword);
if(!resultPassword){
$(this).next('span').html(' the
→ password must contain at least
→ 1 upper case character, 1 lower
→ case character, 1 number and 1
→ special character and must be
→ at least 8 characters long')
.css({'color': '#FF0000'});
} else {
$(this).next('span').html('');
}
});
```

2. Save the jQuery file and place it on your web server. Load **comments.html** into your browser.

3. Select subscriber from the drop-down list to enable the password field. Type in a password and tab or click away from the field. If the password doesn't meet the criteria, an error message is delivered .

When the blur event handler is called on the password field, the function gets the value of the password field and assigns it to the variable **thisPassword**. The variable containing the password's value is then tested against the regular expression to determine whether the password contains all of the necessary parts to make a strong password.

Working with a form has been fun, but let's turn our focus to something a lot more visual. For the next several exercises, you'll build and enhance a photo gallery.

B Oops! A bad password reveals a really long error message.

Using and Updating Attributes

In many of the exercises in the first couple of chapters, you've seen just how handy an attribute can be, because many of the elements you selected used an attribute selector (you'll learn more about attribute selectors in Chapter 5, "Harnessing Advanced Selectors") like this one:

```
$('element[name="element_name"]')
```

Having the ability to identify and set attributes makes it easy for developers to add jQuery interactions to existing websites where the markup has long been established. On existing sites you may not have to edit your existing markup in order to add jQuery.

To get started you'll get the **alt** attribute from the image tags in the library and display them as image titles.

Using the attr( ) method to get an attribute's information:

1. Open a fresh copy of the **html5_boilerplate.html** file in your IDE and add the following markup to create a list of images:

```
<ul class="imageGallery">
<li><img src="images/
→ thumb_lv01.jpg" alt="Classic
→ Sign - Las Vegas" />
</li>
<li><img src="images/
→ thumb_lv02.jpg" alt="New York
→ New York - Las Vegas"/>
</li>
<li><img src="images/
→ thumb_lv03.jpg" alt="Neon
→ Lights - Las Vegas" />
</li>
<li><img src="images/
→ thumb_lv04.jpg" alt=
→ "Stratosphere -  Las Vegas" />
</li>
<li><img src="images/
→ thumb_lv05.jpg" alt="Wynn
→ Hotel - Las Vegas" />
</li>
<li><img src="images/
→ thumb_lv06.jpg" alt=
→ "Paris - Las Vegas" />
</li>
</ul>
```

2. Save the file as **gallery.html** (Script **3.3.html**). Upload the file to your web server; you should see the plain gallery **Ⓐ**.

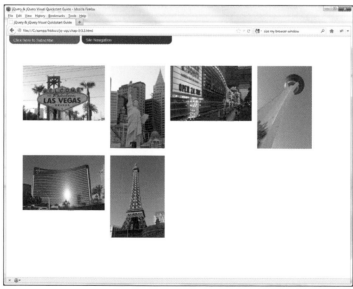

Ⓐ The starting point for the photo gallery.

Classic Sign - Las Vegas

New York New York - Las Vegas

B The **alt** attribute values have been used to set the titles for the pictures.

3. Add the following code to the **jquery.custom.js** file to get the value of the **alt** attribute:

```
$('.imageGallery li img')
.each(function() {
var thisAltTag =
  $(this).attr('alt');
$(this).parent().append('<br />
  <span class="imageTitle">' +
  thisAltTag + '</span>');
});
```

Once you've gotten the **alt** attribute information from each image (using **each()**, a jQuery utility function covered in Chapter 9, "Turning on jQuery's Utilities"), you can append it to the list item. (There's more about **append()** in Chapter 4, "Manipulating DOM Elements.") You also used the **parent()** method, which allows you to traverse the DOM tree. You'll learn more about **parent()** in Chapter 6, "Traversing the DOM Tree."

4. Save **jquery.custom.js**, upload it to your web server, and reload **gallery.html** in your browser. You should see titles under your pictures **B**.

It's just as easy to add and set attributes, and the syntax is exactly the same for both operations. You'll do both in the same exercise but just by modifying the function in the previous exercise.

To set and add attributes using attr():

1. Make the following modifications (highlighted) to the jQuery function you created in the previous exercise:

```
$('.imageGallery li img')

.each(function() {

var thisAltTag =
➝$(this).attr('alt');

$(this).attr({

'alt': thisAltTag +
➝'<br />by Jay Blanchard ',

'data-camera': 'Canon 7D'

});

var newAltTag =
➝$(this).attr('alt');

var cameraTag =

$(this).attr('data-camera');

$(this).parent()

.append('<br /><span class=
➝"imageTitle">' + newAltTag +
➝'</span>');

$(this).parent()

.append('<br /><span class=
➝"imageCamera">' + cameraTag +
➝'</span>');

});
```

2. Upload the jQuery file to the web server and reload **gallery.html** in your browser. If everything was successful, you'll see the updated **alt** attribute and new **data-camera** attribute you added **C**.

3. View the HTML in your DOM inspection tool and you should see the modified markup **D**.

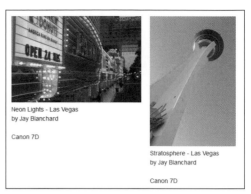

Neon Lights - Las Vegas
by Jay Blanchard

Canon 7D

Stratosphere - Las Vegas
by Jay Blanchard

Canon 7D

C The text from the modified **alt** attribute and the new **data-camera** attribute are visible.

```
<!DOCTYPE html>
<html lang="en">
  <head>
  <body>
    <div id="registration">
    <div id="navigation">
    <div id="content">
      <ul class="imageGallery">
        <li>
        <li>
        <li>
          <img alt="Neon Lights - Las Vegas<br />by Jay Blanchard
          " src="images/thumb_lv03.jpg" data-camera="Canon 7D">
          <br>
          <div class="imageTitle">
          <br>
          <div class="imageCamera">Canon 7D</div>
        </li>
        <li>
          <img alt="Stratosphere - Las Vegas<br />by Jay Blanchard
          " src="images/thumb_lv04.jpg" data-camera="Canon 7D">
          <br>
          <div class="imageTitle">
          <br>
          <div class="imageCamera">Canon 7D</div>
        </li>
        <li>
        <li>
      </ul>
    </div>
  </body>
</html>
```

D The markup has been modified in the DOM.

JavaScript Object Literals

Quite simply, a JavaScript Object Literal is a list of name-value pairs wrapped in a set of curly braces. Each name-value pair is separated by a comma, and each pair describes a property of an object.

Here's an example of how an object can be declared with certain properties in place:

```
var person = {
'name': 'Jay',
'location': 'Texas',
'occupation': 'developer'};
```

There should be no comma after the last property. Each property for the person is then accessible using the syntax **person.name** (which returns Jay) or **person.occupation** (which returns developer).

In JavaScript and jQuery, the JavaScript Object Literal is a handy way to store properties for use with functions. You'll see them used extensively as you learn jQuery.

You can change or set any number of attributes in one call to the **attr()** method just as you did in this exercise. By including each attribute name and value in a map (see the sidebar "JavaScript Object Literals") surrounded by curly brackets, it's possible to set or add as many attributes as you need for the job at hand.

```
{'name': 'value', 'name': 'value', ...}
```

TIP Quotes around attribute names are optional with the exception of the class attribute, where quotes are required.

TIP When you view the source of the browser page, you're viewing the markup in the original state it was in after it was requested from the server. The source never changes; you must use a DOM inspector to see updates you make with jQuery.

You should be fairly comfortable with getting and modifying values, properties, and attributes at this point. The methods for working with values, attributes, and properties are straightforward and feature a clean syntax for getting, adding, and setting each effectively.

Handling CSS Classes

We briefly touched on creating styles using the **css()** method in the first couple of chapters—but what if you have a more complicated class that you'd like to keep encapsulated within your CSS files? The jQuery library has four methods that work with the class attribute of any element. They are **addClass()**, **removeClass()**, **hasClass(),** and **toggleClass()** (see Table 3.1).

Let's explore using each of these methods, starting with **addClass()**.

To use the addClass() method:

1. Add the following code to your **jquery. custom.js** file. Each line adds a class or classes (which have already been defined in the **css/base.css** file) to specific elements in the photo gallery:

```
$('.imageGallery li img')
.addClass('imageBoxShadow');
$('.imageCamera')
.addClass('blueBoxShadow
 small_text');
```

2. Save the jQuery file and place it on the web server. Load **gallery.html** (which did not have to be modified) into your web browser. The result is that the image and camera information have had complex classes applied to them 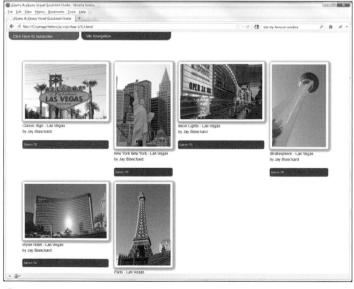.

You'll notice two things about these lines of jQuery code. The first is that a complex selector was used to grab the first group of elements (the images in the list), and the second is that two classes were added to the second set of elements, the items identified by the class **imageCamera**.

The selector in the first line allows you to target a specific group of elements (images in a specific list) to which you'll add a class

Ⓐ Pictures with style!

without requiring you to change your markup. The jQuery library read selectors like this from right to left: "select all images that are children of list items in a container having the **imageGallery** class."

The **addClass()** method in the second line shows you how to add multiple classes to the selected elements. You can add any number of classes to an element or set of elements.

TIP CSS styles are where browsers tend to differ most. Be sure to check your classes in multiple browsers to make sure they are applied as you desire them to be.

TIP Don't use jQuery to add all of your styles in a web page. Doing so would be inefficient and a management nightmare.

TIP Because jQuery reads selectors from right to left, be careful with the use of lengthy selectors. The jQuery team continues to make selectors like this more efficient.

To use the removeClass() method:

1. Add a hover event handler to the jQuery file to remove the **small_text** class from the camera information:

```
$('.imageCamera')
.hover(function() {
$(this)
.removeClass('small_text');
}, function() {
$(this).addClass('small_text');
});
```

2. Upload the saved jQuery file to the web server and reload **gallery.html** in your browser. Use your mouse cursor to hover over the camera information **div** and you'll see the text become larger **B**.

continues on next page

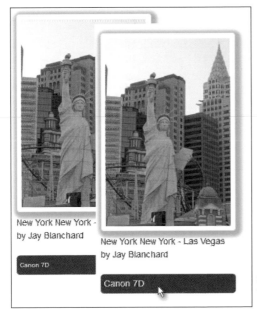

New York New York - by Jay Blanchard

Canon 7D

New York New York - Las Vegas by Jay Blanchard

Canon 7D

B The small text class is removed and the text reverts to its normal size, making the information easier to read.

On occasion you'll need to know if an element has a certain class applied to it. For example, a large-scale website might have a class applied to the body element and the developer will use the existence of the class to determine what, if any, actions may be permitted while the class exists on the body element. The **hasClass()** method is perfect for testing to see whether the class exists on the element. The function will return true if the class exists, false if not.

To use the hasClass() method:

1. Add the following test condition to check the unordered list to see if it has the class **imageGallery**:

   ```
   if(true == $('ul')
   .hasClass('imageGallery')) {
   console.log('ul has the
   ➝imageGallery class');
   } else {
   console.log('ul does not have the
   ➝imageGallery class');
   }
   ```

2. Save the **jquery.custom.js** file and upload it to the proper place on your web server.

3. You're only logging the results for the test, so check the console log tool in your web development tools to see if the message exists ⓒ.

Although this exercise is just a small example of how to test with the **hasClass()** method, you'll no doubt find better ways to use the function as your jQuery skills grow.

The ability to turn a class on and off easily is a piece of cake for the jQuery **toggleClass()** method. Let's look at one way to apply the **toggleClass()** method.

ⓒ The **imageGallery** class is on the unordered list, as shown in Firebug's console log.

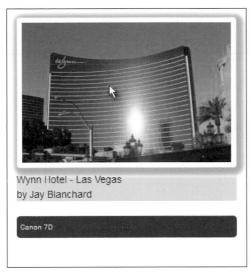

Wynn Hotel - Las Vegas
by Jay Blanchard

Canon 7D

D The highlighted text can be turned on or off.

To use the toggleClass() method:

1. Modify **jquery.custom.js** to add the following function, which will trigger turning a highlight on or off on the picture's title when clicked:

```
$('.imageGallery li img')
.click(function() {
$(this)
.parent()
.find('.imageTitle')
.toggleClass('textHighlight');
});
```

2. Save the jQuery file to your web server and reload **gallery.html** in your web browser.

3. Click on one or more of the pictures in the browser and the title text for the picture will either have the **highlight** class applied or removed **D**.

In this exercise you used two DOM traversal methods, **parent()** and **find()**. You'll learn more about those in Chapter 6.

Any of the class methods can be used to act on multiple classes, a great feature to have packed into your development toolbox. The CSS attribute functions allow you to construct complex classes in your CSS files, which you can then use in your jQuery code while keeping code organization clean.

The jQuery attribute manipulators give you unprecedented power over values, properties, and attributes associated with your markup elements. Take a few moments to review what you've learned so far and then strap in for more DOM manipulation excitement!

Rewind and Review

Take a few moments to reflect on what you've learned in this chapter:

- What is the difference between an attribute and a property?

- Why is an input "type" considered a property?

- When you declare a custom attribute (HTML5), what must the name of the attribute begin with?

- Can you name all of the Boolean properties available for HTML elements?

- What is a JavaScript Object Literal?

- In which direction does jQuery read selectors?

- What properties should you never remove from the DOM?

- Why is a DOM inspection tool, like Firebug, important?

- How could the `hasClass()` method come in handy in the `toggleClass()` example?

4

Manipulating DOM Elements

Adding, changing, and removing elements from your web pages based on user interactions is one of the coolest things you can do with jQuery. The library is deep, with lots of functions you can apply to your web pages to achieve dramatic effects.

In many of the exercises prior to this chapter, you've used the **css()** method to create styles on the fly. In this chapter, you'll take it a couple of steps further using CSS height, width, and position properties. You've also used the **html()** method to add error messages when form elements were not filled out correctly. You'll explore using **html()** further while employing some custom HTML attributes.

The DOM manipulators don't stop there. You'll learn how to copy, add, change, and remove DOM elements to enhance your website visitors' experience. Let's get started!

In This Chapter

Inserting Elements

You'll find there are times when you need to add and remove elements from your web pages. The jQuery library provides a number of methods for performing these manipulations, allowing you a great deal of flexibility when creating specific interactions (see **Table 4.1**).

Of special note are the methods that perform the same function but use a different syntax. Take, for example, **before()** and **insertBefore()**. Both allow you to place content into your page in the same way but with the syntax flipped:

```
$('element')
    .before('<p>before element</p>');
$('<p>before element</p>')
    .insertBefore('element');
```

The paragraph containing "before element" will be inserted before "element" in either case—the choice for you is a stylistic one. Many say using **insertBefore()** is more easily read because it reads left to right and is easier to understand. On the other hand, many like the syntax of the first example even if it's another case where jQuery sounds a little like Yoda. Methods that perform the same task are pointed out in their descriptions.

TABLE 4.1 DOM Insertion Manipulators

Method	Use It To...
after()	Insert content after each of the selected elements.
insertAfter()	Perform the same action as after(); requires a different syntax.
append()	Insert content at the end of each selected element.
appendTo()	Perform the same task as append(), but the syntax is flipped.
prepend()	Insert content at the beginning of each selected element.
prependTo()	Perform the same task as prepend(), but the syntax is reversed.
before()	Insert content before each of the selected elements.
insertBefore()	Perform the same action as before(), but the syntax is flipped.
clone()	Create a deep copy (copies all of the descendants) of the set of selected elements.
detach()	Remove the set of matched elements from the DOM and keep the data for later reinsertion.
empty()	Remove all child nodes of the set of selected elements from the DOM.
remove()	Remove the set of selected elements from the DOM.
removeAttr()	Remove an attribute from each of the selected elements.
replaceAll()	Replace each target element with the set of selected elements.
replaceWith()	Replace each element in the set of selected elements with new content.
wrap()	Wrap an HTML structure around each element in the set of selected elements.
unwrap()	Remove the parents of the set of selected elements from the DOM.
wrapAll()	Wrap an HTML structure around all elements in the set of selected elements.
wrapInner()	Wrap an HTML structure around the content of each element in the set of selected elements.

Creating a Lightbox Effect

In the next few exercises you'll use several of the DOM manipulators to create a lightbox effect. Many websites use a lightbox effect to show enlargements of photographs centered and highlighted on web pages. You'll be able to use the effect on your web pages too, once you've learned how to put together the function.

Some of the manipulators that you'll use during the exercise are specifically designed for getting or modifying information about CSS. These are described in **Table 4.2**.

The first order of business is covering the current page with a translucent background on which the photograph will be displayed.

TABLE 4.2 DOM CSS Manipulators

Method	Use It To...
`css()`	Get or set the value of a style property for the first element in the set of selected elements.
`height()`	Get the current computed height for the first element in the set of selected elements.
`innerHeight()`	Get the current computed height for the first element in the set of selected elements, including the padding but not the border.
`outerHeight()`	Get the current computed height for the first element in the set of selected elements, including padding, border, and optionally, margin.
`width()`	Get the current computed width for the first element in the set of selected elements.
`innerWidth()`	Get the current computed width for the first element in the set of selected elements, including the padding but not the border.
`outerWidth()`	Get the current computed width for the first element in the set of selected elements, including padding and border.
`offset()`	Get the current coordinates of the first element in the set of selected elements, relative to the document.
`position()`	Get the current coordinates of the first element in the set of selected elements, relative to its parent element.
`scrollLeft()`	Get the current number of pixels hidden from view to the left of any scrollable area for the first element in the set of selected elements.
`scrollTop()`	Get the number of pixels hidden above any scrollable area for the first element in the set of matched elements.
`remove()`	Remove the set of selected elements from the DOM.
`removeAttr()`	Remove an attribute from each of the selected elements.
`replaceAll()`	Replace each target element with the set of selected elements.
`replaceWith()`	Replace each element in the set of selected elements with new content.
`wrap()`	Wrap an HTML structure around each element in the set of selected elements.
`unwrap()`	Remove the parents of the set of selected elements from the DOM.
`wrapAll()`	Wrap an HTML structure around all elements in the set of selected elements.
`wrapInner()`	Wrap an HTML structure around the content of each element in the set of selected elements.

To use the append() method to display a translucent shade:

1. Open **gallery.html** in your text editor and add the **data-photo** attribute to each of the list items (Script **4.1.html**):

```
<li>
<img src="images/thumb_lv01.jpg"
→ data-photo="images/lv01.jpg"
→ alt="Classic Sign - Las Vegas" />
</li>
<li>
<img src="images/thumb_lv02.jpg"
→ data-photo="images/lv02.jpg" alt=
→ "New York New York - Las Vegas" />
</li>
<li>
<img src="images/thumb_lv03.jpg"
→ data-photo="images/lv03.jpg"
→ alt="Neon Lights - Las Vegas" />
</li>
<li>
<img src="images/thumb_lv04.jpg"
→ data-photo="images/lv04.jpg" alt=
→ "Stratosphere -  Las Vegas" />
</li>
<li>
<img src="images/thumb_lv05.jpg"
→ data-photo="images/lv05.jpg"
→ alt="Wynn Hotel - Las Vegas" />
</li>
<li>
<img src="images/thumb_lv06.jpg"
→ data-photo="images/lv06.jpg"
→ alt="Paris - Las Vegas" />
</li>
```

2. Save the **gallery.html** file and upload it to your web server.

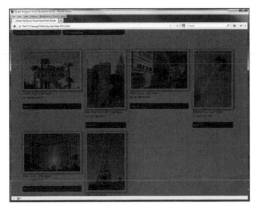

A The backdrop is in place for the lightbox.

B The backdrop **div** element is the last element within the body tags.

3. Edit **jquery.custom.js** and insert the following code to add a translucent background to the browser window:

```
$('.imageGallery li img')
.click(function() {
$('body').append
('<div class="shade"></div>');
$('.shade')
.css('opacity', 0.7).fadeIn();
});
```

4. Save the jQuery file and upload it to your server.

5. Click on any of the images in the photo gallery and the background should appear. There's no way to get rid of it at this point without reloading the page. You'll add code to remove it later **A**.

For the backdrop to appear, you have to append a **div** to the body element of your page and declare the shade class on the **div** (the shade class is already defined for you in **css/base.css**). At this point, you apply a CSS opacity property (to make the backdrop translucent) and use **fadeIn()** to bring the backdrop into view. (More on **fadeIn()** and other effects in Chapter 8, "Creating Captivating Effects.")

Take a look at your DOM inspection tool while you have the **div** applied to the body. Notice that the backdrop **div** is the last element within the body tags because **append()** inserts content at the end of the selected element **B**.

With the backdrop in place, it's time to add the photo. There will be two things you'll have to take care of: preloading all the full-sized images and placing the image centered on the browser window.

continues on next page

The reason for preloading the images is to ensure that the lightbox function can properly measure the image and know how to place it within the window. The jQuery methods can't get the height and width of an element that isn't currently available in the DOM. Failing to perform this step results in the image not being centered properly .

C The top-left corner of the image is centered on the screen rather than the whole photo.

You'll also use the browser window's height to set the size of the image to make sure the photo is fully displayed within the boundaries of the browser window. Many of the full-sized images in the example are either taller or wider than the browser window **D**.

As a matter of organization, most developers will group functions like the image preloader near the top of their jQuery file. In this case, the preloader needs to have completed its job before the lightbox function is called, so let's put the preloading function together first.

To create an image preloader using appendTo():

1. Edit your jQuery file to add the image preloader:

```
function preload(arrayOfImages) {
$(arrayOfImages).each(function(){
$('<img />')
.attr('src',this)
.appendTo('body')
.css('display','none');
});
}
```

You start by declaring a function named **preload**. The function is given the argument of **arrayOfImages**. Once the

D You can never tell how tall the Statue of Liberty is until you try to fit her in a browser window.

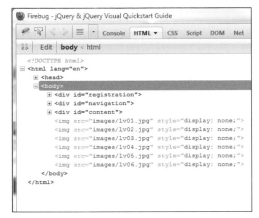

E The new image tags have been appended to the body.

function is called, the jQuery method **each()** loops through each item in the array that you'll pass to the function. (More on **each()** in Chapter 9, "Turning on jQuery's Utilities.")

For each image, you append an image tag to the body. Then you set the **src** attribute for the image tag to the current image information. Finally, you make sure the images are not visible until you need them by setting their CSS display method to **none**.

Using **appendTo()** here makes perfect sense because it allows you to specify attributes more easily for each image tag prior to the tag being added to the page.

2. Create the array inside a function call to **preload**:

```
preload([
        'images/lv01.jpg',
        'images/lv02.jpg',
        'images/lv03.jpg',
        'images/lv04.jpg',
        'images/lv05.jpg',
        'images/lv06.jpg'
]);
```

The square brackets indicate a JavaScript array using JavaScript Object Notation. The path for each full-sized image has been specified in a comma-separated list. Have a look at your DOM inspector and you should see the image tags just before the closing body tag **E**.

Now let's add further to the lightbox function.

To use height() and width() to set an element's size and position:

1. Open **jquery.custom.js** in your text editor.

2. Add the following jQuery code to create an image tag:

```
var imgSRC = $(this)
→.attr('data-photo');

var imgTAG =
→'<img src="'+ imgSRC + '" />';
```

This code should be added immediately after the line where you applied **fadeIn()** to the backdrop.

3. Continue the function by adding the following code to append the modal window to the body and the image tag to the modal window:

```
$('body')
.append('<div class="photoModal">
</div>');
$('.photoModal').html(imgTAG);
$('.photoModal')
    .fadeIn('slow')
    .append('<div>
<a href="#" class="closePhoto">
Close X</a></div>');
```

The additional **append()** method adds an anchor tag to the modal, which will be used for closing the photo.

4. Enter the code to check the window's height and apply the height to the image:

```
var windowHeight =
↪$(window).height();
$('.photoModal img')
.css('height',
     (windowHeight - 200));
```

You've subtracted 200 pixels from the window's height to ensure that the image will fit in the browser window.

5. Save information about the modal's current height and width to two variables.

These two variables will be applied to the modal to center it horizontally and vertically within the browser window:

```
var modalTopMargin =
↪($('.photoModal')
     .height() + 20) / 2;
var modalLeftMargin =
↪($('.photoModal')
     .width() + 20) / 2;
```

The reason you add 20 to the height and width is because the CSS specified for the modal window has a border of 10 pixels per side **F**.

continues on next page

F Take note of the border to make sure the photo is perfectly centered.

6. Add the code to apply the CSS to the modal:

```
$('.photoModal')
.css({
  'margin-top' : -modalTopMargin,
  'margin-left': -modalLeftMargin
});
```

In the original CSS (see **css/base.css**) for the modal, the top-left corner is originally set to be in the center of the screen. The top-left corner of the browser window is at coordinates 0, 0 .

To make sure the photo is centered, you apply negative measurements from the photo's top-left corner to move it into position .

G The base coordinates for the browser window start at the upper-left corner.

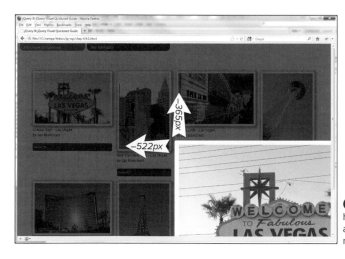

H By calculating the photo's height and width, you can apply negative numbers to move it into position.

7. Save the jQuery file and upload it to your web server. Reload gallery.html into your web page and click on one of the pictures 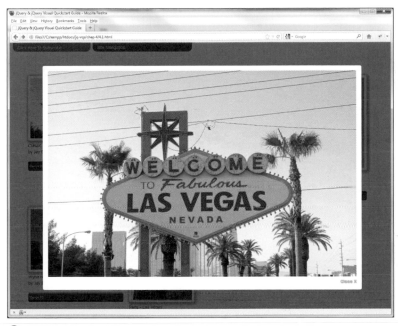.

There's only one problem at this point: you can't close a picture once you've opened it. Because you've added elements to the DOM that were not previously there, you'll have to use a special way to attach event handlers to account for the new elements.

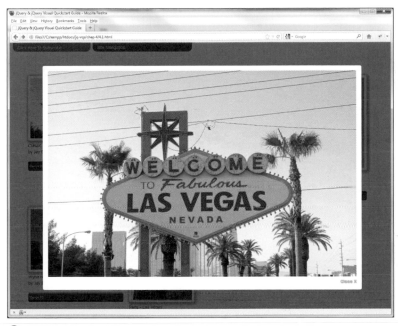

I The picture is sized and presented!

To close the picture using remove():

1. Reload **jquery.custom.js** into your text editor.

2. Add the following function to the file:

```
$('body')
.on('click', '.closePhoto',
→ function(e){
e.preventDefault();
$('.photoModal, .shade')
    .fadeOut(function(){
        $(this).remove();
    });
});
```

The **on()** method accounts for elements either in the DOM now or added in the future. You use it to bind event handlers to items within a selected element. In the exercise, you attached the click event handler to the body and specified that the handler should answer to any item having the **closePhoto** class. You'll recall that you appended an anchor

tag having the class **closePhoto** in the previous exercise.

Once the tag is clicked, the photo modal and the backdrop are faded and then removed using the **remove()** method, allowing the lightbox function to be reset for its next performance.

You have undoubtedly noticed the **preventDefault()** method used here. You passed the click event e to the function:

```
function(e){...}
```

To keep the link from acting normally, which is typically navigating to another page, you applied the **preventDefault()** method to the event, which does what it says—it prevents the default event action from occurring.

3. Save the file and upload it to your web server.

4. Reload the **gallery.html** page. Click on an image and then click on the "Close X" link at the bottom right of the image. Your gallery page has returned to normal.

More Fun with DOM Manipulators

Let's look at more ways to use some of the other DOM manipulators.

To use before( ) to rearrange order:

1. Open a new copy of the HTML5 boilerplate in your text editor and add the following markup (Script **4.2.html**):

```
<div id="content>
<div class="article">
<h3>Article 1</h3>
<p>Lorem ipsum...</p>
<a href="" class="mover">
move to top</a></div>
<div class="article">
<h3>Article 2</h3>
<p>Lorem ipsum... </p>
<a href="" class="mover">
move to top</a></div>
```

```
<div class="article">
<h3>Article 3</h3>
<p>Lorem ipsum...</p>
<a href="" class="mover">
move to top</a></div>
<div class="article">
<h3>Article 4</h3>
<p>Lorem ipsum...</p>
<a href="" class="mover">
move to top</a></div>
<div class="article">
<h3>Article 5</h3>
<p>Lorem ipsum...</p>
<a href="" class="mover">
move to top</a></div>
</div>
```

2. Save the file as **article.html** and upload it to your web server. Load the page into your browser 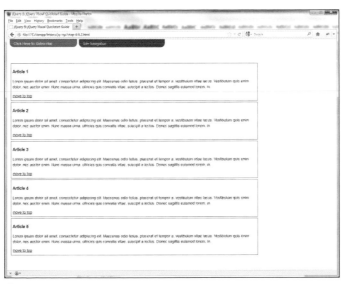.

continues on next page

Ⓐ The list of articles in their normal order.

3. Modify **jquery.custom.js** with the following code to move an article to the top of the list of articles:

```
$('.mover').click(function(e) {

e.preventDefault();

$('#content div:first')

.before($(this).parent('div'));

});
```

4. Save the jQuery file and upload it to your web server.

5. Reload **article.html** in your web browser and click on any of the "move to top" links. The article moves to the top of the list **B**.

Let's look at what's in play here. Using **before()** makes things read backward so the selector selects the first **div**, using a jQuery selector extension (more about those in Chapter 5, "Harnessing Advanced Selectors"), **:first**. The first **div** in the group is the **div** you'll insert your chosen **div** before. Whew. Then you invoke the **before()** method to carry your chosen **div** to the first spot in the group **C**.

To get the chosen **div**, you get the parent **div** of the clicked link. The **parent()** method is a DOM traversal method you'll see again in Chapter 6, "Traversing the DOM Tree."

The **before()** method has a counterpart that performs the same job exactly, the **insertBefore()** method. The **insertBefore()** method has one huge advantage: It's much easier to read:

```
$(this).parent('div')

.insertBefore($('#content div:first'));
```

This line of code says to take the clicked element's parent **div** and insert it before the first **div** in the selected group of **div**s. Which one should you use? As mentioned earlier, it's a matter of personal preference.

B You can rearrange the list to bring an article to the top.

C Clicking the third **div** moves it to the top of the list.

Getting and Setting Measurements

There are some DOM manipulators whose sole purpose is to help you get and set measurements. Let's use a couple of those to help animate a floating menu.

To use scrollTop() and offset() to create a floating menu:

1. Modify the markup of **article.html** first by adding a **div** to wrap the **div** with an **id="content"** (Script **4.3.html**):

```
<div class="pageWrapper">
<div id="content">
// all of the content is here
</div>
</div>
```

2. Add the following markup to define the floating menu. It must be within the **pageWrapper div**:

```
<div class="sidebar">
<a href="article.html">
Articles</a><br />
<a href="gallery.html">
Photo Gallery</a>
</div>
```

3. Save **article.html** and upload it to your web server.

4. Create the jQuery function to make the menu float in **jquery.custom.js**:

```
var sidebarOffset =
  $('.sidebar').offset();
var paddingTop = 10;
$(window).scroll(function() {
if ($(window).scrollTop() >
  sidebarOffset.top) {
$('.sidebar').stop()
.animate({
marginTop: $(window).scrollTop() -
  sidebarOffset.top + paddingTop
});
} else {
$('.sidebar').stop()
.animate({
marginTop: $(window).scrollTop()
});
}
});
```

5. Save **jquery.custom.js** and upload it to your web server.

continues on next page

6. Load **article.html** into your web browser and you'll see the floating menu on the right-hand side of the page **Ⓐ**.

As you scroll down the page, the menu will float into place **Ⓑ**.

Let's see what's behind the curtain on making this little function work. First you save the sidebar's offset to a variable. The **offset()** function gets the current position of an element relative to the document. The function returns an object having two properties: **top** and **left** **Ⓒ**.

Ⓐ The new menu is ready to go.

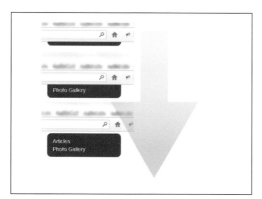

Ⓑ The menu floats into view as lightly as a cloud.

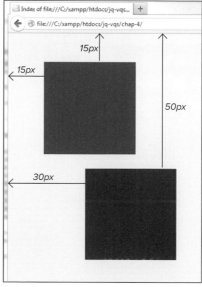

Ⓒ An example of offset for two elements.

The other measurement you took is the window's **scrollTop()** amount. This measurement, in pixels, is the number of pixels hidden from view above the browser window as you scroll down the page **D**.

TIP You can determine the bottom and right properties of an object by using **offset()** and a little math.

Once the scroll event takes place, all you have left to do is to animate the **div** into its new position (you'll read more about animations in Chapter 8). You'll do that based on the measurement provided by **scrollTop()**. Then you do a little math to subtract the original offset amount and add in a padding value to make sure the **div** is 5 pixels below the edge of the top of the browser window **E**.

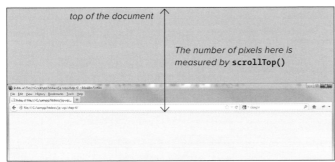

D The **scrollTop()** method measures what you can't see.

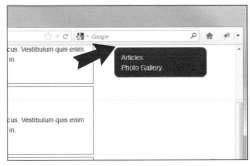

E The original gap is maintained after the animation.

Cloning

You should be getting pretty comfortable manipulating elements in the DOM. You've learned how to add and remove elements, get measurement information, and set measurement information. Let's turn our focus to duplicating elements on a page, a little thing jQuery calls *cloning*.

On the surface, cloning a group of elements on a page looks pretty simple. All you have to do is use the **clone()** function and you're all set, right? Let's dig a little further.

When you use the **clone()** method, you're making a copy of the selected elements and all of their descendants and any text nodes contained within the selected items and the descendants. This is known as a *deep copy*.

You can also copy the entire set of event handlers bound to the selected elements, ensuring that your functions will continue to work even though you're adding new elements to the DOM. You do this by setting the **withDataAndEvents** and **deepWithDataAndEvents** properties of **clone()** to **true**.

To demonstrate **clone()**, you'll create a new form for the website that allows visitors to submit recipes. Some recipes have more ingredients than others, but you don't want to clutter up the page with input elements. You'll use the **clone()** method to allow form users to add as many ingredient fields as they need.

To use clone() to add form elements:

1. Use a fresh copy of the HTML5 boiler-plate in your text editor and add the following markup to create a recipe form (Script **4.4.html**):

```
<div id="content">
<h2>Submit a recipe...</h2>
<form name="recipe" action="inc/
→ php/recipe.php" method="post">
<input name="recipeName"
→ placeholder="Recipe Name"/>
<div id="ingredients">
<p>Ingredients</p>
<span class="inputSpan">
<input name="recipeIngredient[]"
→ placeholder="Ingredient" />
<br /></span>
<span class="inputSpan">
<input name="recipeIngredient[]"
→ placeholder="Ingredient" />
→ <br /></span>
<span class="inputSpan">
<input name="recipeIngredient[]"
→ placeholder="Ingredient" /> 
<a href="newIngredient">add
→ another ingredient</a>
<br /></span>
</div>
<p>Instructions</p>
<textarea name=
→ "recipeInstructions">
</textarea><br />
<input type="submit" name="submit"
→ value="Submit Recipe" />
</form>
</div>
```

Submit a recipe...

Recipe Name

Ingredients

Ingredient

Ingredient

Ingredient   add another ingredient

Instructions

Submit Recipe

Ⓐ The new recipe form is almost ready to go.

Take note of the span tags surrounding the inputs for ingredients. These are used to make writing your code much easier and more compact. Additionally, each ingredient tag is named with square brackets (**[]**) to make them each part of an array that can be handled more easily by server-side languages like PHP.

2. Save the file as **recipe.html** and upload it to your web server. When loaded into a browser, it looks like Ⓐ.

3. Add a function to **jquery.custom.js** to clone the last recipe ingredient span:

```
$('a[href="newIngredient"]')
.click(function(e){
e.preventDefault();
var clonedInput =
→ $('.inputSpan').filter(':last')
.clone(true, true);
```

Using a class on the span tags surrounding it helps to keep your selector short. Be sure to set the **clone()** function's properties to **true, true** so event handlers are copied.

4. Get the current value of the last input. You'll use this value to make sure you don't lose any ingredients:

```
var lastInputData = $('input[name=
→ "recipeIngredient[]"]')
.filter(':last').val();
```

continues on next page

5. Set the last ingredient input's HTML to get rid of the link and to ensure that it retains its current value:

```
$('.inputSpan').filter(':last')

.html('<span class="inputSpan">
→ <input name="recipeIngredient[]"
→ placeholder="Ingredient"
→ value="' + lastInputData + '" />
→ <br /></span>');
```

Resetting the HTML of the element prevents it from creating the "add another ingredient" link again and again **B**.

6. Append the cloned input to the ingredients **div**:

```
$('#ingredients')

.append(clonedInput);
```

7. Clean up the new input by setting its value to be blank and then placing the focus on the new input:

```
$('input[name=
→ "recipeIngredient[]"]')

.filter(':last').val('');

$('input[name=
→ "recipeIngredient[]"]')

.filter(':last').focus();

});
```

Setting the focus into the new input is a convenience for users. It allows them to just start typing when the new element is added.

8. Save the jQuery file and upload it to your server. Reload **recipe.html** and click the "add another ingredient" link **C**.

If you keep clicking the link, the click event handler is triggered each time without you having to resort to changing the event handler **D**.

B Duplicating the links not only looks bad, but also it's confusing to the user.

C A new ingredient field has been added and now has the focus.

D The click event is still triggered each time because you set up **clone()** to copy the event handlers for the form.

Chaining jQuery Methods

In many of the exercises in this book, you've used several jQuery methods on a single selector. Using more than one function on a selector is known as *chaining*.

Chaining is beneficial for two reasons. First, you don't have to reselect elements to add another function to them, thus saving time. Second, you can use chaining to make your code much more readable. You're allowed to place line breaks between each function:

```
$('input[name="recipeIngredient[]"]')
    .filter(':last')
    .val('')
    .focus();
});
```

The only caveat with chaining you need to be aware of is function order. Be sure to add functions in the order you wish them to be executed or the results may not be what you expect.

Keep in mind that chaining jQuery functions is not suitable for every situation. There may be times when you need to reselect elements because of the function's length or the order in which you need things to occur. In those cases, you may want to cache a selector by holding it in a variable:

```
var ingredients = $('input[name="recipeIngredient[]"]');
```

The selector **$(ingredients)** is now reusable:

```
$(ingredients)
    .filter(':last')
    .val('')
    .focus();
```

Caching the selector also prevents jQuery from having to reselect the elements each time it's used, providing enhanced performance—especially when there is a large group of elements defined by one selector.

Changing an Input Element

Let's make one other change to the form. Assume the user wants to designate that an ingredient is really a spice. To accomplish the change, you'll use the **replaceWith()** manipulator to change the input.

To use replaceWith() to change an element:

1. Modify the first two ingredient inputs of **recipe.html** to create a link that will trigger the change to a spice, as seen in the following highlighted markup (Script **4.5.html**):

   ```
   <span class="inputSpan">
   <input name="recipeIngredient[]"
     placeholder="Ingredient" />
      <a href="makeSpice"
     class="ingredientType">change
     to spice</a><br /></span>
   ```

2. Save **recipe.html** and upload it to your web server .

Ⓐ The new links have been added to the input boxes.

3. Open **jquery.custom.js** and modify the function you created in the previous exercise to account for the additional link. The section you need to add is highlighted:

```
$('.inputSpan')

.filter(':last')

.html('<span class="inputSpan">
    <input name="recipeIngredient[]"
    placeholder="Ingredient" value=
    "' + lastInputData + '" />
     <a href="makeSpice"
    class="ingredientType">change
    to spice</a><br /></span>');
```

By making this modification, you ensure that the link to change the input element is available.

4. Create a new function in **jquery. custom.js**. The function will determine what kind of input is available and make the needed change:

```
$('#ingredients').on('click',
    '.ingredientType', function(e) {

e.preventDefault();

var ingredientType =
    $(this).attr('href');

if('makeSpice' == ingredientType)
{
```

5. Get the existing value of the input:

```
var oldElement =
    $(this).closest('span');

var oldElementValue =
    $(this).closest('span')

.find('input').val();
```

6. Create the new input element and assign it to a variable to be used later in the function:

```
var newElement =
    '<span class="inputSpan">
    <input name="recipeSpice[]"
    placeholder="Spice" value="' +
    oldElementValue + '" />

 <a href="makeIngredient"
    class="ingredientType">
    change to ingredient</a>
    <br /></span>';
```

7. Replace the old input with the new input:

```
$(oldElement)

.replaceWith(newElement);
```

8. Set the new input's value based on what was already entered in the form:

```
$(newElement).find('input')

.val(oldElementValue);
```

continues on next page

9. Add the remainder of the function to change the input back to an ingredient input if requested:

```
else {
var oldElement =
→ $(this).closest('span');
var oldElementValue =
→ $(this).closest('span')
.find('input').val();
var newElement =
'<span class="inputSpan">
→ <input name="recipeIngredient[]"
→ placeholder="Ingredient"
→ value="' + oldElementValue
→ + '" /> 
→ <a href="makeSpice"
→ class="ingredientType">change
→ to spice</a>
<br /></span>';
$(oldElement)
.replaceWith(newElement);
$(newElement).find('input')
.val(oldElementValue);
}
});
```

The functionality of the **else** condition is exactly the same as the **if** condition, except that it changes the input type back to ingredient.

10. Save **jquery.custom.js** and upload it to your web server. Reload **recipe.html** in your browser and click one of the "change to spice" links **B**.

TIP When you add an ingredient, the creation of another input element occurs and has the "change to spice" link added **C**.

B The input has been changed to reflect its status as a spice.

C New inputs have been added, ready to take their place in the recipe as an ingredient or a spice.

Take a look at your DOM inspection tool, and you'll see the changes you put into place **D**.

There should be no doubt that jQuery makes it very easy to manipulate DOM elements. The library excels at adding, removing, measuring, and changing elements on every web page you create. The library's ability to modify markup is a valuable set of tools that lets you worry less about existing markup—giving you the power to make sensible changes that will allow your functions to operate effectively.

You also learned how to chain jQuery methods to create complex functions. Chaining makes your code compact, easy to read, and efficient.

Next you're going to ramp up your understanding and use of selectors. Selector boot camp ahead!

```
<div id="ingredients">
    <p> Ingredients </p>
    <span class="inputSpan">
    <span class="inputSpan">
        <input placeholder="Ingredient" name="recipeIngredient[]">
        <a class="ingredientType" href="makeSpice"> change to spice </a>
        <br>
    </span>
    <span class="inputSpan">
</div>
```

D The replaced input elements are evident when inspecting the DOM.

Rewind and Review

Take a few moments to reflect on what you've learned in this chapter:

- How many of jQuery's DOM manipulators have counterpart functions that perform the same action?

- Are there advantages to using functions that perform the same action but have a different syntax? What are the advantages?

- Why is it a good idea to preload images?

- What is the benefit of using a DOM inspection tool like Firebug?

- What is **preventDefault()** used for?

- What is the difference between **postion()** and **offset()**?

- How do you preserve event handlers on cloned elements?

- How does the term deep copy apply to cloned elements?

- When should you cache a selector?

- How many jQuery functions can you chain together?

- Are line breaks allowed when chaining jQuery methods?

Harnessing
Advanced Selectors

In each of the exercises to this point, you've mostly used jQuery's basic selectors to identify elements you've wanted to work with. The basic selectors have worked well and will continue to serve most of your needs.

You've also used one of the more advanced selectors, an attribute selector. These types of selectors identify the element and then a particular attribute that the element has, such as `$('a[href="foo.html"])`. But there's a lot more you can do with attribute selectors, such as selecting attributes that start or end with a particular value or contain a certain word. Many of the attribute selectors offer regular expression–like functionality.

You can create powerful AND/OR conditions when using attributes to do your selecting. In this chapter, you'll learn how to set up those conditions and combine selectors to get the elements you're looking for when applying jQuery's methods.

Forming Attribute Selectors

The jQuery attribute selectors (listed in Table 5.1) are designed to help you be able to select elements according to the various attributes you may put into element tags. They're all based on CSS selector syntax with the exception of one, the *not equal* selector.

The *not equal* selector is another of jQuery's selector extensions. It allows you to create a selector that either has attributes without a particular value or doesn't have the attribute at all.

Typically, you'll use the attribute selectors by starting with an element and then following it up with the attribute and the value that you're looking for. Here's an example of the syntax:

`$('img[src="images/foo.jpg"]')`

First you stated that you were looking for an image and that the image tag should have the attribute `src` with a value of `"images/foo.jpg"`. An element is not required to use an attribute selector. One of the reasons for using an attribute selector, instead of an ID or a class, is that you can do so when you don't have the ability to make changes to the markup.

Quotes are important in the attribute selectors, and I'm using a quote order that was preferred beginning in jQuery version 1.5. To me it looks natural because most developers place double-quotes around their attribute values in the markup. You aren't restricted to using this quote order, but you must use quotation marks when specifying attribute selectors.

The first exercise will teach you how to use the substring selector to identify articles by the same author. Are you ready to get started on using the attribute selectors? Let's go!

TABLE 5.1 jQuery Attribute Selectors

Syntax	What It Selects
`[name|="value"]`	Elements that have an attribute containing a prefix. The prefix may also be followed by a hyphen (-).
`[name*="value"]`	Elements that have an attribute that contains a particular substring.
`[name~="value"]`	Elements that have an attribute value containing a particular word, where the word is delimited by spaces.
`[name$="value"]`	Elements that have an attribute value ending exactly with a given string.
`[name="value"]`	Elements that have an attribute value exactly equal to the given value.
`[name!="value"]`	Elements that either don't have the specified attribute or do have the specified attribute but not with a particular value. This is a jQuery extension.
`[name^="value"]`	Elements that have an attribute value beginning exactly with the given string.
`[name]`	Elements that have the specified attribute, with any value.

To use [name*="value"] to find a substring:

1. Open your saved **article.html** in your text editor and add the highlighted markup to the first five article **div**s (Script **5.1.html**; the full paragraphs are not shown in the exercise for the sake of brevity and to eliminate unnecessary greeking):

```
<div class="article">
<h3>Article 1</h3>
<p class="by-line">
<span data-author="Blanchard, Jay"
→ class="author">Jay Blanchard
→ </span>
 posted: 
<span data-date="2012-08-16"
→ class="postDate">August 16, 2012
</span></p>
<p>Lorem ipsum ... </p>
<a href="" class="mover">
move to top</a></div>
<div class="article">
<h3>Article 2</h3>
<p class="by-line">
<span data-author="Castro, Jesse"
→ class="author">Jesse Castro
→ </span>
 posted: 
<span data-date="2012-06-18"
→ class="postDate">June 18, 2012
</span></p>
<p>Lorem ipsum... </p>
<a href="" class="mover">
move to top</a></div>
<div class="article">
<h3>Article 3</h3>
```

```
<p class="by-line">
<span data-author="Awl, Dave"
→ class="author">David Awl</span>
 posted: 
<span data-date="2012-05-07"
→ class="postDate">May 7, 2012
</span></p>
<p>Lorem ipsum... </p>
<a href="" class="mover">
move to top</a></div>
<div class="article">
<h3>Article 4</h3>
<p class="by-line">
<span data-author="Blanchard, Jay"
→ class="author">Jay Blanchard
→ </span>
 posted: 
<span data-date="2012-02-03" class
→ ="postDate">February 3, 2012
</span></p>
<p>Lorem ipsum... </p>
<a href="" class="mover">
move to top</a></div>
<div class="article">
<h3>Article 5</h3>
<p class="by-line">
<span data-author="Castro, Jesse"
→ class="author">Jesse Castro
→ </span>
 posted: 
<span data-date="2012-02-02"
→ class="postDate">February 2,
→ 2012</span></p>
<p>Lorem ipsum... </p>
<a href="" class="mover">
move to top</a></div>
```

continues on next page

2. Save the file and upload it to your web server. Once it's loaded in the browser, you'll see the byline for each article .

3. Add the following function to your **jquery.custom.js** file starting with the initial selector:

```
$('.author').hover(function(){
```

4. Capture the value of the custom attribute containing the author's name:

```
thisAuthor = $(this)
    .attr('data-author');
```

5. Create an array containing the author's last name and first name by using the JavaScript **split** function. You'll be using the author's last name in the substring attribute selector:

```
authorNameArray = thisAuthor
    .split(',');
authorLastName =
→ authorNameArray[0];
```

6. Set up the substring attribute selector using the author's last name:

```
$('.author[data-author*="'
→ + authorLastName + '"]')
    .addClass('textHighlight');
```

7. Complete the second half of the hover function by removing the added class **textHighlight** from every element in the **author** class:

```
}, function(){
$('.author')
    .removeClass('textHighlight');
});
```

Article 1

Jay Blanchard posted: August 16, 2012

Lorem ipsum dolor sit amet, consectetur adipiscing elit. Maecenas odio tellus, placerat et tempor a, vestibulum vitae lacus. Vestibulum quis enim dolor, nec auctor enim. Nunc massa urna, ultricies quis convallis vitae, suscipit a lectus. Donec sagittis euismod lorem, in.

move to top

Article 2

Jesse Castro posted: June 18, 2012

Lorem ipsum dolor sit amet, consectetur adipiscing elit. Maecenas odio tellus, placerat et tempor a, vestibulum vitae lacus. Vestibulum quis enim dolor, nec auctor enim. Nunc massa urna, ultricies quis convallis vitae, suscipit a lectus. Donec sagittis euismod lorem, in.

move to top

Article 3

David Awl posted: May 7, 2012

Lorem ipsum dolor sit amet, consectetur adipiscing elit. Maecenas odio tellus, placerat et tempor a, vestibulum vitae lacus. Vestibulum quis enim dolor, nec auctor enim. Nunc massa urna, ultricies quis convallis vitae, suscipit a lectus. Donec sagittis euismod lorem, in.

move to top

Article 4

Jay Blanchard posted: February 3, 2012

A All of the articles now how have bylines with post times.

8. Place the `jquery.custom.js` file on your web server and reload `article.html` in your web browser. Hover over an author's name and you should see the name highlighted in all of the articles written by this author **B**.

Being able to target a portion, or substring, within an attribute value is especially valuable when adding jQuery to sites that already exist. By studying the existing markup, you can look for cases where using the substring attribute selector will work perfectly for your needs.

In the next exercise, you'll add some keywords to each article so you can perform a similar search to determine which articles have the same tags applied to them. For this you'll use the word attribute selector.

To use the [name~=value] attribute selector:

1. Modify the markup in `article.html` (Script `5.2.html`) to add the tags for each article, as highlighted here:

```
<div class="article">

<h3>Article 1</h3>

<p class="by-line">

<span data-author="Blanchard, Jay"
→ class="author">Jay Blanchard

</span>

 posted: 

<span data-date="2012-08-16"
→ class="postDate">August 16, 2012

</span></p>

<p>Lorem ipsum...</p>

<a href="" class="mover">

move to top</a>
```

continues on next page

Article 1

Jay Blanchard posted: August 16, 2012

Lorem ipsum dolor sit amet, consectetur adipiscing elit. Maecenas odio tellus, placerat et tempor a, vestibulum vitae lacus. Vestibulum quis enim dolor, nec auctor enim. Nunc massa urna, ultricies quis convallis vitae, suscipit a lectus. Donec sagittis euismod lorem, in.

move to top

Article 2

Jesse Castro posted: June 18, 2012

Lorem ipsum dolor sit amet, consectetur adipiscing elit. Maecenas odio tellus, placerat et tempor a, vestibulum vitae lacus. Vestibulum quis enim dolor, nec auctor enim. Nunc massa urna, ultricies quis convallis vitae, suscipit a lectus. Donec sagittis euismod lorem, in.

move to top

Article 3

David Awl posted: May 7, 2012

Lorem ipsum dolor sit amet, consectetur adipiscing elit. Maecenas odio tellus, placerat et tempor a, vestibulum vitae lacus. Vestibulum quis enim dolor, nec auctor enim. Nunc massa urna, ultricies quis convallis vitae, suscipit a lectus. Donec sagittis euismod lorem, in.

move to top

Article 4

Jay Blanchard posted: February 3, 2012

Lorem ipsum dolor sit amet, consectetur adipiscing elit. Maecenas odio tellus, placerat et tempor a, vestibulum vitae lacus. Vestibulum quis enim dolor, nec auctor enim. Nunc massa urna, ultricies quis convallis vitae, suscipit a lectus. Donec sagittis euismod lorem, in.

B All of the author's articles are highlighted.

```
 Tags:<span data-tags=
→"JavaScript jQuery Scripting"
→class="articleTags">

<span>JavaScript</span>
→<span>jQuery</span>
→<span>Scripting</span>

</span>

</div>

<div class="article">

<h3>Article 2</h3>

<p class="by-line"><span data-
→author="Castro, Jesse" class=
→"author">Jesse Castro</span>

 posted: 

<span data-date="2012-06-18"
→class="postDate">June 18, 2012

</span></p>

<p>Lorem ipsum... </p>

<a href="" class="mover">

move to top</a>

 Tags:<span data-tags="PHP
→MySQL" class="articleTags">

<span>PHP</span> <span>MySQL</span>

</span>

</div>

<div class="article">

<h3>Article 3</h3>

<p class="by-line">

<span data-author="Awl, Dave"
→class="author">David Awl</span>

 posted: 

<span data-date="2012-05-07"
→class="postDate">May 7, 2012

</span></p>

<p>Lorem ipsum... </p>

<a href="" class="mover">

move to top</a>
```

```
 Tags:<span data-tags=
→"Social Media Facebook Twitter"
→class="articleTags">

<span>Social Media</span>
→<span>Facebook</span>
→<span>Twitter</span></span>

</div>

<div class="article">

<h3>Article 4</h3>

<p class="by-line"><span data-
→author="Blanchard, Jay" class=
→"author">Jay Blanchard</span>

 posted: 

<span data-date="2012-02-03"
→class="postDate">February 3,
→2012

</span></p>

<p>Lorem ipsum... </p>

<a href="" class="mover">move to
→top</a>

 Tags:<span data-tags=
→"JavaScript jQuery HTML5 CSS3"
→class="articleTags">

<span>JavaScript</span>
→<span>jQuery</span>

<span>HTML5</span>

<span>CSS3</span>

</span>

</div>

<div class="article">

<h3>Article 5</h3>

<p class="by-line"><span data-
→author="Castro, Jesse" class=
→"author">Jesse Castro</span>

 posted: 

<span data-date="2012-02-02" class=
→"postDate">February 2, 2012

</span></p>
```

```
<p>Lorem ipsum... </p>

<a href="" class="mover">move to
→ top</a>

 Tags:<span data-tags=
→ "PHP jQuery HTML5"
→ class="articleTags">

<span>PHP</span>

<span>jQuery</span> <span>HTML5
→ </span>

</span>

</div>
```

2. Upload the **article.html** file to your web server and load it into your browser to see the article tags **C**.

3. Prepare for the function by binding a hover event handler to the tags:

```
$('.articleTags span')

    .hover(function(){
```

4. Get the text from the span the user is currently hovering over:

   ```
   thisTag = $(this).html();
   ```

5. Create the word attribute selector using the value from the current span. Use the **parent()** and **find()** traversal methods (more on those in Chapter 6, "Traversing the DOM Tree") to identify the article's title. Then apply the **textHighlight** class to the titles:

   ```
   $('[data-tags~="'

   + thisTag + '"]')

   .parent('.article')

   .find('h3')

   .addClass('textHighlight');
   ```

   continues on next page

C The article tags are now in place.

6. Complete the hover function by removing the **textHighlight** classes when the mouse isn't hovering over one of the tags:

```
},function(){
    $('.article h3')
    .removeClass('textHighlight');
});
```

7. Save and upload the **jquery.custom.js** file to the web server and reload **article.html** in your web browser. Hover over a tag and note that the titles are highlighted .

The word attribute selector looks for single words surrounded by white spaces. You may have noticed during your testing that there's a problem with one of the tags. The Social Media tag contains two words. The solution to that problem will be revealed in the section "Combining Selectors" later in this chapter.

But before we move on to combining selectors, let's take a look at the jQuery extension for attribute selectors, the *not equal* selector.

D Hovering over a tag reveals other articles containing the same tag.

To use the [name!=value] selector:

1. Add a custom attribute to the h3 tags in **article.html** (Script **5.3.html**). Do not modify any of the rest of the markup. For the sake of clarity only the h3 tags are shown here, with the modification highlighted:

```
<h3 data-title="Article 1">
    Article 1</h3>
<h3 data-title="Article 2">
    Article 2</h3>
<h3 data-title="Article 3">
    Article 3</h3>
<h3 data-title="Article 4">
    Article 4</h3>
<h3 data-title="Article 5">
    Article 5</h3>
<h3 data-title="In other news...">
    In other news...</h3>
```

   Adding these custom attributes doesn't change the look of the page 🅒.

2. Bind the header tag for each article to the hover event handler by adding the following to the **jquery.custom.js** file:

```
$('.article h3')
.hover(function(){
```

3. Get the value of the h3's text and place it into a variable called **thisTitle**:

```
var thisTitle = $(this).html();
```

4. Create the *not equals* attribute selector and select all h3s not equal to the h3 currently being hovered over. Find the parent article **div** for each one and fade its opacity to make it less visible:

```
$('h3[data-title!="'
→ + thisTitle + '"]')
.parent('.article')
.fadeTo(350, 0.4);
```

   The **parent()** function belongs to the DOM traversal methods and the **fadeTo()** method is one of jQuery's special effects that you'll learn more about in Chapter 8, "Creating Captivating Effects."

5. Complete the function by having the *mouseout* side of the hover event handler fade all of the articles back to normal:

```
}, function(){
    $('.article').fadeTo(250, 1.0);
});
```

continues on next page

6. Upload **article.html** and **jquery. custom.js** to your web server. Load **article.html** into your browser and hover the cursor over an article title .

Pretty neat! All of the other article information is faded, drawing more attention to the currently chosen article with just a few lines of jQuery code and the powerful *not equals* attribute selector. You'll undoubtedly find many uses for this selector.

Sometimes you need something more powerful for a selector because of the way your web pages are constructed or to handle specific tasks within your pages. With jQuery you can combine attribute selectors and use them to gain the power necessary to construct a selector that will solve your most complex problems. Let's dive into that next.

Ⓔ The focus is placed on the current article's information.

Combining Selectors

The attribute selectors are jQuery's only selectors that allow you to create and use an OR condition. Consider the following selector where you might want to affect two or more elements having different classes:

```
$('.class_A, .classB')
```

Essentially you're saying that you've selected **class_A** AND **class_B** by placing a comma between each class name. You can do this with any of the normally combined selectors. If you leave a space between the classes, like this:

```
$('.class_A .class_B')
```

you're indicating that you want to select all **class_B** elements that are children of **class_A** elements.

With attribute selectors you can utilize an OR condition by placing a comma between the selectors:

```
$('[name~="foo"],[name~="bar"])
```

Combining the attribute selector in this case says select elements with the word "foo" OR "bar" in the attribute's value. Removing the comma creates an AND condition.

Let's modify the function that uses tags to determine which article titles to highlight so that it will handle two word tags, like "Social Media."

To combine attribute selectors for an OR condition:

1. Modify `article.html` (Script **5.4.html**) to add a Media-only tag to Article 5, as highlighted here:

```
<span data-tags="PHP jQuery HTML5
 Media" class="articleTags">
<span>PHP</span>
<span>jQuery</span>
<span>HTML5</span>
 <span>Media</span>
</span>
```

continues on next page

2. Place **article.html** on your web server and load it into your browser to confirm that the new tag is in place .

3. Open **jquery.custom.js** in your text editor and edit the function that highlights article titles when a tag is hovered on. First, leave the initial binding in place:

```
$('.articleTags span')
.hover(function(){
```

4. Leave the variable assignment holding the HTML from the tag alone:

```
var thisTag = $(this).html();
```

5. Add a JavaScript **split** function that will divide all words in the tag by a space:

```
var tagArray = thisTag
    .split(' ');
```

6. Test the array created by the **split** function to see if its length is two words:

```
if(2 == tagArray.length) {
```

7. Set up the OR condition for attribute selectors (in this case, a word selector) to handle each word in the array. The traversal and class additions remain the same:

```
$('[data-tags~=
→"' + tagArray[0] + '"],
[data-tags~=
→"' + tagArray[1] + '"]')
    .parent('.article')
    .find('h3')
    .addClass('textHighlight');
```

8. Configure the else condition:

```
} else {
```

Article 3

David Awl posted: May 7, 2012

Lorem ipsum dolor sit amet, consectetur adipiscing elit. Maece dolor, nec auctor enim. Nunc massa urna, ultricies quis conval

move to top Tags: Social Media Facebook Twitter

Article 4

Jay Blanchard posted: February 3, 2012

Lorem ipsum dolor sit amet, consectetur adipiscing elit. Maece dolor, nec auctor enim. Nunc massa urna, ultricies quis conval

move to top Tags: JavaScript jQuery HTML5 CSS3

Article 5

Jesse Castro posted: February 2, 2012

Lorem ipsum dolor sit amet, consectetur adipiscing elit. Maece dolor, nec auctor enim. Nunc massa urna, ultricies quis conval

move to top Tags: PHP jQuery HTML5 Media

In other news...

Lorem ipsum dolor sit amet, consectetur adipiscing elit. Sed tir faucibus imperdiet. Vestibulum rhoncus dapibus mi, quis luctus sem. Fusce a elit ac metus auctor vulputate. Donec et fringilla

A The Media tag is now in place.

Article 3

David Awl posted: May 7, 2012

Lorem ipsum dolor sit amet, consectetur adipiscing elit. Maecen
dolor, nec auctor enim. Nunc massa urna, ultricies quis convallis

move to top Tags: Social Media Facebook Twitter

Article 4

Jay Blanchard posted: February 3, 2012

Lorem ipsum dolor sit amet, consectetur adipiscing elit. Maecen
dolor, nec auctor enim. Nunc massa urna, ultricies quis convallis

move to top Tags: JavaScript jQuery HTML5 CSS3

Article 5

Jesse Castro posted: February 2, 2012

Lorem ipsum dolor sit amet, consectetur adipiscing elit. Maecen
dolor, nec auctor enim. Nunc massa urna, ultricies quis convallis

move to top Tags: PHP jQuery HTML5 Media

In other news...

Lorem ipsum dolor sit amet, consectetur adipiscing elit. Sed tinc
faucibus imperdiet. Vestibulum rhoncus dapibus mi, quis luctus
sem. Fusce a elit ac metus auctor vulputate. Donec et fringilla n

B The OR condition makes it easy to select the proper titles.

9. Change the original selector by replacing **thisTag** with **tagArray[0]** to handle a one-word tag:

```
$('[data-tags~="' +
→ tagArray[0] + '"]')
.parent('.article')
.find('h3')
.addClass('textHighlight');
}
```

10. Close out the hover event handler by removing the text-highlighting class when the mouse moves away from a tag:

```
},function(){
$('.article h3')
.removeClass('textHighlight');
});
```

11. Upload **jquery.custom.js** to your web server and reload the **article.html** file in your browser. Hover over the Social Media tag and you'll see that its current article title is highlighted as well as the article title having the Media tag **B**.

If you want to make sure that you only get the articles with a Social Media tag (or any other two-word tag), you need to place a comma between the attribute selectors.

Now that you've used several of the attribute selectors, the rest should be easy to implement when you need them. You are now equipped to use all of the selectors in jQuery's arsenal. With that knowledge in hand, it is time to climb another tree—the DOM tree.

Rewind and Review

Take a few moments to reflect on what you've learned in this chapter:

- What's the difference between an AND and an OR condition in a jQuery attribute selector?

- Which of the attribute selectors is a jQuery extension?

- When using attribute selectors, what's the one thing that's required in the selector?

- Are you required to use an element in combination with an attribute selector?

- Is quote order important in attribute selectors?

- What's the syntax for the substring attribute selector?

6

Traversing the DOM Tree

To paraphrase a line from a famous Christmas story, "Yes, Virginia, we can get there from here—even if there are a lot of steps along the way."

Selectors are usually fine for identifying elements that you want to work with while using jQuery, but you'll often find that you need to identify other elements on your pages based on their relationship to the selected elements. These elements might be parents, grandparents, children, or siblings, and the basic concept is that you're moving up, down, and sideways in the family tree (the DOM) based on which limb you're currently standing on (the selected elements). This movement is known as *traversing the DOM tree*. You've seen a couple of examples of this movement in earlier chapters, but now it's time to dig in and learn more about using jQuery's DOM traversal methods.

The jQuery library offers three types of traversal methods: tree traversal, traversal filters, and some miscellaneous methods that don't fit neatly into the other categories. Let's start with tree traversal.

Traversing the Tree

Moving up, down, and sideways through the elements on a web page can be quite an adventure. You'll have to navigate carefully to make sure that you apply your functions to the right elements in the tree. In many of the exercises that you've done to this point, you've seen examples of this navigation, moving around the DOM tree with ease to identify and act on parts of the web pages that you've constructed.

The jQuery library offers several methods (**Table 6.1**) that allow you to perform traversal movements easily. In almost every case, you can get to any element on a page from any other element on the page just by using and combining the right traversal methods in the right order. But be careful. You'll want to be practical in your traversal actions to make your functions easy to maintain and scalable.

In any examination of traversal methods you'll need to be focused on the markup

TABLE 6.1 jQuery Traversal Methods

Function Name	What It Does
children()	Gets the children of each element in the set of matched elements; can be filtered using a selector.
closest()	Gets the first element that matches the selector, beginning at the current element and progressing up through the DOM tree.
find()	Gets the descendants of each element in the current set of matched elements; can be filtered by a selector, jQuery object, or element.
next()	Gets the immediately following sibling of each element in the set of matched elements. If a selector is provided, it retrieves the next sibling only if it matches that selector.
nextAll()	Gets all following siblings of each element in the set of matched elements; can optionally be filtered by a selector.
nextUntil()	Gets all following siblings of each element up to but not including the element matched by the selector, DOM node, or jQuery object passed.
offsetParent()	Gets the closest ancestor element that is absolutely, relatively, or fixed in position (aka a positioned element).
parent()	Gets the parent of each element in the current set of matched elements; can optionally be filtered by a selector.
parents()	Gets the ancestors of each element in the current set of matched elements; can be filtered by a selector.
parentsUntil()	Gets the ancestors of each element in the current set of matched elements, up to but not including the element matched by the selector, DOM node, or jQuery object.
prev()	Gets the immediately preceding sibling of each element in the set of matched elements; can be filtered by a selector.
prevAll()	Gets all preceding siblings of each element in the set of matched elements; can be filtered by a selector.
prevUntil()	Gets all preceding siblings of each element up to but not including the element matched by the selector, DOM node, or jQuery object.
siblings()	Gets the siblings of each element in the set of matched elements, optionally filtered by a selector.

and the code used to move through that markup. The exercises here will reflect that, allowing you to look at how the jQuery code is used to move through the DOM tree.

Let's look at the functions that you've built so far and what made that navigation possible.

To use the next() method:

1. Open Script **6.1.html** in your text editor and locate the lines of markup for the form. In particular, look for input elements that have a span following them **Ⓐ**.

2. Identify the code in **jquery.custom. js** that's used to find out whether the contact name is blank. The lines using the **next()** methods are highlighted:

```
$('input[name="contactName"]')
.focusout(function(){
if(0 -- $(this).val().length) {
$(this).next('span')
.html(' please do not leave
→ name blank')
```

```
.css({
'color': '#FF0000'
});
} else {
$(this).next('span').html('');
}});
```

The **next()** function identifies the span that's the sibling of the input element **Ⓑ**.

The **next()** method identifies the element immediately following the selected element because it's a sibling. As long as the selected item and the selected item in the **next()** method are on the same level, the method will find the sibling that follows the selected item.

The **prev()** method works in the opposite direction, finding siblings that come before the selected elements. The **siblings()** method works in both directions from the element that you have selected.

TIP Indentation in your markup can help you to locate ancestors, descendants, and siblings easily.

```
<form name="contact" action="inc/php/contact.php" method="post">
    <input type="text" name="contactName" placeholder="your name"/><span></span><br />   ◄ • • • • • • • • •
    <input type="text" name="contactEMail" placeholder= "your e-mail address"/><span></span><br />◄ • • • •
    <textarea name="contactComments" placeholder="your comments"></textarea><br />
    <button type="submit" name="submit">Send your comments</button>
</form>
```

Ⓐ The markup for the form inputs with their span sections attached.

```
<input type="text" name="contactName" placeholder="your name"/><span></span><br />
```

Ⓑ The next-door neighbor of the input element is the span that directly follows it.

Finding ancestors (parents, grandparents, etc.) is just as easy to do with the proper traversal method. Let's find an immediate parent first.

To use the parent() method:

1. Load Script **6.2.html** into your web browser. You'll be working with the list of images to find their parents **C**.

2. Open **jquery.custom.js** and find the code block used to add information to each image. The lines using the **parent()** method have been highlighted:

```
$('.imageGallery li img')

.each(function() {

var thisAltTag =
  → $(this).attr('alt');

$(this).attr({

'alt': thisAltTag +

'<br />by Jay Blanchard ',

'data-camera': 'Canon 7D'

});
```

```
var newAltTag =
  → $(this).attr('alt');

var cameraTag =
  → $(this).attr('data-camera');

$(this).parent()

.append('<br /><div
  → class="imageTitle">'
  → + newAltTag + '</div>');

$(this).parent()

.append('<br /><div class=
  → "imageCamera">' + cameraTag +
  → '</div>');

});
```

The new information could be appended to the image tag, but that would make the information part of the image tag itself and not visible to the website visitor. The best way to handle the additional information is to append it to the list item. The list item is the parent of the image, so you can use the **parent()** method to specify that the additional information is added to the list item **D**.

```
<ul class="imageGallery">
    <li><img src="images/thumb_lv01.jpg" alt="Classic Sign - Las Vegas" /></li>
    <li><img src="images/thumb_lv02.jpg" alt="New York New York - Las Vegas" /></li>
    <li><img src="images/thumb_lv03.jpg" alt="Neon Lights - Las Vegas" /></li>
    <li><img src="images/thumb_lv04.jpg" alt="Stratosphere - Las Vegas" /></li>
    <li><img src="images/thumb_lv05.jpg" alt="Wynn Hotel - Las Vegas" /></li>
    <li><img src="images/thumb_lv06.jpg" alt="Paris - Las Vegas" /></li>
</ul>
```

C The markup for the image list.

```
<li><img src="images/thumb_lv02.jpg" alt="New York New York - Las Vegas" /></li>
```

D Finding the parent of the image.

A single element can hold any number of elements, sometimes many layers deep. Let's look at a way to find an element's parent and then locate another element that is a descendant of the parent.

To use the find() method to locate a child element:

1. Open Script **6.3.html** in your browser and then look at the markup in a DOM inspection tool like Firebug. The element **<div class="imageTitle">** that you're searching for was added when the page loaded and is highlighted here **E**:

```
<li>
<img class="imageBoxShadow"
→ alt="Classic Sign - Las Vegas
<br />by Jay Blanchard "
data-photo="images/lv01.jpg"
→ src="images/thumb_lv01.jpg"
→ data-camera="Canon 7D">
<br>
<div class="imageTitle">
Classic Sign - Las Vegas
<br>
by Jay Blanchard
</div><br>
<div class="imageCamera
→ blueBoxShadow small_text">
Canon 7D</div>
</li>
```

2. Locate the section of jQuery in the **jquery.custom.js** file used to highlight the image title when the image is clicked:

```
$('.imageGallery li img')
.click(function() {
$(this).parent()
.find('.imageTitle')
.toggleClass('textHighlight');
});
```

When the click event handler is called in the jQuery function you created, the parent of the image (the list item) is located first. From there you used the **find()** method to locate the child element of the list item having a class of **imageTitle** **F**.

You use **find()** by including a selector, in this case a class name, for an element that you expect to be a descendant of the original selector.

```
<li>
    <img class="imageBoxShadow" alt="Classic Sign - Las Vegas<br />by Jay Blanchard
    <div class="imageTitle">Classic Sign - Las Vegas<br>by Jay Blanchard</div><br>
    <div class="imageCamera blueBoxShadow small_text">Canon 7D</div>
</li>
```

E The markup was modified on page load to add the image title and other information.

```
•••• <li>
•••••► <img class="imageBoxShadow" alt="Classic Sign - Las Vegas<br />by
        <div class="imageTitle">Classic Sign - Las Vegas<br>by Jay Blancha
        <div class="imageCamera blueBoxShadow small_text">Canon 7D</div>
    </li>
```

F You ascend the DOM tree to the parent element and then descend from the parent to find the descendant that you're looking for.

More than one jQuery method is available to find an ancestor element similar to **parent()**. The **closest()** method can help you pinpoint a specific ancestor—the closest ancestor to the selected element. To see how that works, let's look at the recipe form that you created in a previous exercise.

To use closest( ) to find an ancestor:

1. Open the **recipe.html** file (Script **6.4.html**) in your text editor and in your browser ⓖ.

2. Find the markup that describes the inputs for the list of ingredients. One of the spans is shown here:

   `<span class="inputSpan">`

   `<input name="recipeIngredient[]"`
   `→ placeholder="Ingredient" />`

   ` <a href="makeSpice"`
   `→ class="ingredientType">`

   `change to spice</a><br /></span>`

3. Locate the function that you created that changes an ingredient input to a spice input. Within that function take note of the following two lines:

   `var oldElement =`
   `→ $(this).closest('span');`

   `var oldElementValue =`
   `→ $(this).closest('span')`

   `.find('input').val();`

Submit a recipe...

Recipe Name

Ingredients

Ingredient	change to spice
Ingredient	change to spice
Ingredient	add another ingredient

Instructions

Submit Recipe

ⓖ To change an ingredient to a spice, you'll have to locate the link's closest span element.

To make this function work, you need to replace an entire span and copy the value of the input contained within that span if a value exists. You use the **closest()** method and specify a selector that says you're looking for the closest span that is an ancestor of the link you clicked .

To make this function work, you need to replace an entire span and copy the value of the input contained within that span if a value exists. You use the **closest()** method and specify a selector that says you're looking for the closest span that is an ancestor of the link you clicked **H**.

In the next line you perform the same action to find the ancestor and then use **find()** to identify the child input and place its value into a variable **I**.

Keep in mind that you don't have to type the syntax in the jQuery as it's shown for the second line. Because you have placed **$(this).closest('span')** in the variable **oldElement**, you can use the following when finding the input and its value:

```
var oldElementValue =
→ $(oldElement).find('input').value();
```

It's easy to navigate the DOM with jQuery's traversal methods, especially if you think of your markup as a tree-like diagram. In more complex markup, it's often helpful to make sure that you maintain consistent tabs and even print your markup and draw the arrows when needed.

Among the jQuery traversal methods are some filter functions that can slice, dice, map, and much more! No, it's not a late-night commercial for some product that you can't live without; it's the jQuery traversal filters. We'll look at those in the next section.

```
<span class="inputSpan"><input name="recipeIngredient[]" placeholder="Ingredient" /> <a href="makeSpice"
```

H The path to the closest span.

```
<span class="inputSpan"><input name="recipeIngredient[]" placeholder="Ingredient" />
```

I Descending the DOM tree to find the input value.

Applying Traversal Filters

Just like filters for selectors, jQuery offers a number of filters (see **Table 6.2**) to assist you in navigating your page markup. In earlier chapters, you were shown how to use one of these methods, `filter()`, to increase performance when using jQuery's selector filter extensions.

Most of the traversal filters have one goal: to reduce the number of elements selected to those fitting a certain criterion. Two of the filters, `is()` and `map()`, have other purposes.

Each of the filtering methods creates a new jQuery object that consists of the elements selected and filtered. The `is()` method does not create a new object, but it does allow you to test the contents of any jQuery object.

TABLE 6.2 jQuery Traversal Filters

Function Name	What It Does
`eq()`	Matches an element at the specified index.
`filter()`	Reduces the set of matched elements to those that match the selector or pass the function's test.
`first()`	Reduces the set of matched elements to the first in the set.
`has()`	Reduces the set of matched elements to those that have a descendant that matches the selector or DOM element.
`is()`	Checks the current matched set of elements against a selector, element, or jQuery object and returns true if at least one of these elements matches the given arguments.
`last()`	Reduces the set of matched elements to the final one in the set.
`map()`	Passes each element in the current matched set through a function, producing a new jQuery object containing the return values.
`slice()`	Reduces the set of matched elements to a subset specified by an index range.

The map() function allows you to apply a function to each element in your selected set. A new jQuery object is created, and it contains the return values from your function.

The miscellaneous traversal methods don't fit neatly into the other categories of jQuery's traversal methods, but they provide unquestionable power when used properly.

To begin your exploration of the traversal filters, let's look at how you can use the eq() method to identify a specific item in a group of elements. Along the way you'll use one of the miscellaneous traversal methods (see **Table 6.3**), not(), to assist in locating and filtering your results.

TABLE 6.3 jQuery Miscellaneous Traversal Methods

Function Name	What It Does
add()	Adds elements to the set of matched elements.
andSelf()	Adds the previous set of elements on the stack to the current set.
contents()	Gets the children of each element in the set of matched elements, including text nodes.
end()	Ends the most recent filtering operation in the current chain and returns the set of matched elements to its previous state.
not()	Removes elements from the set of matched elements.

To use the eq( ) method:

1. Create a new HTML page (Script **6.5.html**) and insert the following table data into the content area:

```
<h3>Products</h3>
    <table id="product_table">
    <thead>
        <tr>
            <th>Date</th>
            <th>Water Pistols</th>
            <th>Balloons</th>
            <th>Party Packs</th>
            <th>Streamers</th>
            <th>Total Shipped
             ·Today</th>
        </tr>
    </thead>
    <tbody >
        <tr>
            <td>2002-03-01</td>
            <td>270</td>
            <td>352</td>
            <td>368</td>
            <td>360</td>
            <td>1350</td>
        </tr>
        <tr>
            <td>2002-03-02</td>
            <td>250</td>
            <td>212</td>
            <td>374</td>
            <td>310</td>
            <td>1146</td>
        </tr>
        <tr>
            <td>2002-03-03</td>
            <td>167</td>
            <td>208</td>
            <td>421</td>
            <td>311</td>
            <td>1107</td>
        </tr>
        <tr>
            <td>2002-03-04</td>
            <td>165</td>
            <td>223</td>
            <td>404</td>
            <td>297</td>
            <td>1089</td>
        </tr>
        <tr>
            <td>2002-03-05</td>
            <td>115</td>
            <td>214</td>
            <td>409</td>
            <td>301</td>
            <td>1039</td>
        </tr>
        <tr>
            <td>Total By Items
             · </td>
            <td>967</td>
            <td>1209</td>
            <td>1976</td>
            <td>1279</td>
            <td> </td>
        </tr>
    </tbody>
    </table>
```

2. Save the file as **products.html** and upload to your web server **A**.

3. Open **jquery.custom.js** in your text editor and start a function that will highlight column totals when an item is hovered over:

```
$('#product_table th')
.not(':first-child, :last-child')
.hover(function(){
```

Since the first column and last column don't have totals associated with them, you've specified that the selector ignore the first and last table head items by using the first and last child selector filters.

4. Using jQuery's **index()** method, get the numerical index of the item being hovered over and place it into a variable:

```
var thisIndex = $(this).index();
```

5. Create a selector for the last row of the table using the **eq()** method. Traverse the row to find the table cell having the same numerical index as the header. Once found, add a class to the cell to highlight the text:

```
$('tr').eq(6)
.find('td').eq(thisIndex)
.addClass('textHighlight');
```

If you physically counted the rows in the table, you know that there are seven

rows. The **eq()** method uses a zero-based index, which is why you'll seek out row number 6.

Keep in mind that under most circumstances, especially when you have dynamically generated elements like table rows, you'll count the rows programmatically, assign that number to a variable, and use that variable in place of the hard-coded number value. Doing so will make your code flexible and more importantly, scalable.

The column headers also have an index, which is the value that you've stored in the **thisIndex** variable and then used to define which of the table cells on the last row will get the class added.

6. Close out the hover function by removing the highlight class from the table cell that has it when the mouse moves away from the header cell:

```
}, function(){
$('td').removeClass
 ('textHighlight');
});
```

7. Save the **jquery.custom.js** file and upload it to your web server. Reload the products page in your browser and hover over the table headers to see the values become highlighted **B**.

continues on next page

Products					
Date	Water Pistols	Balloons	Party Packs	Streamers	Total Shipped Today
2002-03-01	270	352	368	360	1350
2002-03-02	250	212	374	310	1146
2002-03-03	167	208	421	311	1107
2002-03-04	165	223	404	297	1089
2002-03-05	115	214	409	301	1039
Total By Items	967	1209	1976	1279	

A The table that you'll be working with.

Products					
Date	Water Pistols	Balloons	Party Packs	Streamers	Total Shipped Today
2002-03-01	270	352	368	360	1350
2002-03-02	250	212	374	310	1146
2002-03-03	167	208	421	311	1107
2002-03-04	165	223	404	297	1089
2002-03-05	115	214	409	301	1039
Total By Items	967	1209	1976	1279	

B Wow! That's a lot of balloons!

You've performed some fairly heavy-duty DOM traversal and filtering to get the results you were looking for. Let's add a wrinkle to the report and find a way to highlight the totals in the last column when the dates are hovered over. You'll need to keep the first and last table rows from being able to run the hover event. Normally this would be a complex operation, but jQuery makes it simple with the `slice()` method.

The `slice()` method uses a zero-based index for counting as well, but it also includes the ability to define an endpoint in the count. For instance, you can apply a style to all of the rows not including the first and last rows by using `slice()` like this 🅲:

🅲 Slicing your way to highlighted rows.

Products					
Date	Water Pistols	Balloons	Party Packs	Streamers	Total Shipped Today
2002-03-01	270	352	368	360	1350
2002-03-02	250	212	374	310	1146
2002-03-03	167	208	421	311	1107
2002-03-04	165	223	404	297	1089
2002-03-05	115	214	409	301	1039
Total By Items	967	1209	1976	1279	

```
$('#product_table tr')

.slice(1, 6)

.find('td').addClass('textHighlight');
```

You must keep in mind that the second number of the `slice()` function defines the point at which elements should stop being selected. Counting the table rows again, you'll see that there are five rows with data and the last row containing data has an index of 5. The first number of the function is inclusive, and the second number is not, which is why 6 was the index defined for the second argument in the function.

Products

Date	Water Pistols	Balloons	Party Packs	Streamers	Total Shipped Today
2002-03-01	270	352	368	360	1350
2002-03-02	250	212	374	310	1146
2002-03-03	167	208	421	311	1107
2002-03-04	165	223	404	297	1089
2002-03-05	115	214	409	301	1039
Total By Items	967	1209	1976	1279	

D Highlighting the total number of goodies shipped on a given day.

Let's set up a hover function for the rows.

To use the slice() function:

1. Edit **jquery.custom.js** to start the function to highlight the last column of a row when the date is hovered over. First, slice the number of rows that you want to work with. Then find the table cell in that row to bind the hover event handler to:

```
$('#product_table tr')

.slice(1, 6)

.find('td:first-child')

.hover(function(){
```

2. Find this table cell's parent because it's the parent of all of the table cells in this row. Find the sixth child (index 5) and add the highlighting class to that child:

```
$(this).parent().find('td').eq(5)

.addClass('textHighlight');
```

3. Close out the hover function by removing the highlight class from the table cell when the **mouseout** event occurs:

```
}, function(){

$('td').removeClass
 ('textHighlight');

});
```

4. Save the jQuery file and upload it to your web server. Reload the **product. html** page in your browser and hover over one of the dates **D**.

Being able to move easily through the DOM elements makes jQuery's traversal methods well worth the time to learn them. You'll find yourself using the DOM traversal and filter methods over and over again.

Rewind and Review

Take a few moments to reflect on what you've learned in this chapter:

- What is a zero-based index?

- How many different groups of traversal methods does the jQuery library offer? How are they divided into groups?

- What is an element right next to another element on the same level called?

- What is the first ancestor of any HTML page? (Hint: You use it when making sure that the page has loaded.)

- What kind of formatting will help you to better visualize the relationships of elements?

- Ancestors move you up the DOM tree; descendants move you down. What moves you sideways in the DOM tree?

- What argument in the **slice()** method is not inclusive?

- Why are chaining jQuery methods so valuable in DOM traversal?

- What method can you use to find the numerical index of any element on a web page?

7

Using Ajax

Of all of the technologies to surface in recent years, there may be none more exciting and useful than Ajax, or Asynchronous JavaScript and XML. Unfortunately, Ajax may have also been one of the most frustrating technologies. Different browsers utilized different syntax and methods in order to achieve the same purpose, and developers found themselves creating large, complex functions to deal with the differences.

The advent of the jQuery library erased the headaches of dealing with Ajax by making it simpler to understand and use. The jQuery team also saw fit to add several shorthand Ajax methods, like **get()** and **post()**, to fit particular needs without having to construct more complex functions to send and retrieve information from web servers.

In this chapter, the focus will be on the shorthand methods. You'll also learn to work with the JSON (JavaScript Object Notation) data that many websites are using to share information. Let's get started.

Applying Shorthand Methods

The beauty of jQuery's Ajax shorthand methods is their simplicity and the fact that their function names focus on what the method is best suited for (**Table 7.1**). Keep in mind that all of the shorthand methods are designed to send request information, including data when needed, to the web server.

It's critical when working with Ajax requests that you have an application that will allow you to observe the request to the server and the response the server returns. There are many good tools available for all of the web browsers, but during the exercises I've used Firebug (available from http://getfirebug.com). The console is easy to understand and provides immediate feedback when performing Ajax requests 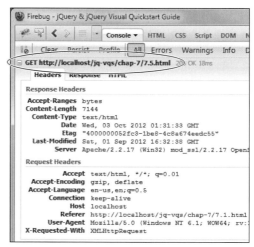.

In the website that you're building, you'll be using Ajax to get content from other pages into the main page and to process forms. Let's start with page loading.

> **TIP** Not all web browsers will execute Ajax requests when loading files locally. Always use a web server when testing Ajax to make sure that Ajax requests are handled properly.

TABLE 7.1 jQuery Ajax Shorthand Methods

Function Name	What It Does
get()	Loads data from the server using an HTTP GET request.
getJSON()	Loads JSON-encoded data from a server using an HTTP GET request.
getScript()	Loads a JavaScript file from the server using an HTTP GET request, and then executes the script file immediately.
load()	Loads data from the server and places the returned HTML into the matched element.
post()	Loads data from the server using an HTTP POST request.

A The Firebug console showing an HTTP request to a web server.

To use the load() method:

1. Create a new **index.html** file (Script **7.1.html**) that has all of the menu elements, including the floating menu :

```
<!DOCTYPE html>
<!--[if lt IE 7 ]>
<html class="ie ie6" lang="en">
 <![endif]-->
<!--[if IE 7 ]>
<html class="ie ie7" lang="en">
 <![endif]-->
<!--[if IE 8 ]>
<html class="ie ie8" lang="en">
 <![endif]-->
<!--[if (gte IE 9)|!(IE)]
><!--><html lang="en">
<!--<![endif]-->
<head>
<meta charset="utf-8">
<title>jQuery &amp; jQuery Visual
 Quickstart Guide</title>
<meta name="description"
 content="">
<meta name="author" content="">
```

continues on next page

B The new index file is ready to go to work.

```
<!-- CSS -->
<link rel="stylesheet"
→ href="css/base.css">


<!-- JAVASCRIPT / JQUERY -->
<!--[if lt IE 9]>
<script src="http://html5shim.
→ googlecode.com/svn/trunk/
→ html5.js">
</script>
<![endif]-->
<script
src="inc/jquery/jquery-1.7.2.js">
</script>
<script src="inc/jquery/jquery.
→ custom.js"></script>
</head>
<body>
<div id="registration">
<form action="inc/php/
→ registration.php" method="post">
<input type="text" name=
→ "userEMail" placeholder="your
→ e-mail address" />
<button type="submit">Subscribe
→ </button>
</form>
<a href="">
Click Here to Subscribe</a>
</div>
<div id="navigation">
<a href="content_index.html">
Home</a>
<a href="content_product.html">
Products</a>
<a href="content_services.html">
Services</a>
<a href="content_about.html">
About Us</a><br />
<span id="drawer_title">
Site Navigation</span>
</div>
<div class="pageWrapper">
<!-- CONTENT -->
<div id="newContent"></div>
<div class="sidebar">
<a href="article.html">
Articles</a><br />
<a href="gallery.html">
Photo Gallery</a><br />
<a href="recipe.html">Recipes</a>
</div>
</div>
</body>
</html>
```

Of special note here is an additional **div** (highlighted) that will hold all of the new content loaded into the page. Also, in the downloadable code, the pages **article.html**, **gallery.html**, and **recipe.html** all retain numerical designations. The markup described here will work with the files as they were named during previous exercises.

2. Upload **index.html** to your web server.

3. Add the following code to **jquery.custom.js** to create a function that handles click events from the floating menu:

```
$('.sidebar a')

.click(function(e) {

e.preventDefault();
```

4. Create the Ajax load function to place the content of the called page into the proper **div** on the calling page:

```
var loadHREF =

$(this).attr('href');

$('#newContent')

.load(loadHREF + ' #content');

});
```

You're first getting the **href** attribute of the link, which is then used to identify the page that you're loading. Second, you identify the element in the called page that you want to place into the element on the calling page.

5. Place the **jquery.custom.js** file in the appropriate location on your web server and reload **index.html** in your web browser.

6. Click any of the links in the floating menu and the content will be loaded into **index.html** **C**.

continues on next page

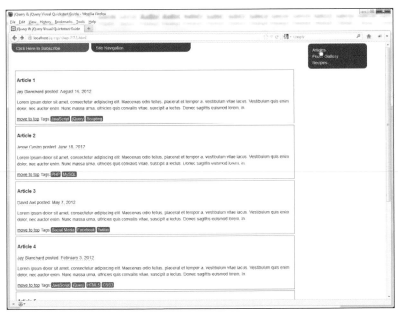

C The new content is loaded into the page.

When you use **load()**, you request the information and place it into an element on the page that you called the function from. The **load()** method also allows you to specify that a specific portion of the loaded page be placed into the element, which is what you've done here. You're not really interested in loading all the content into your existing page, so you specified the ID of the element on the remote page, which should be shown within the **newContent div D**.

TIP By properly using variables and setting up your jQuery functions to use them, you can keep your functions short and able to handle changes to the markup. If you add more pages to this site and more links in the floating menu, this function needs no modification to handle the new content.

Note: Scripts 7.2 through 7.5 in the code that you can download from the book's companion site (www.jayblanchard.net) are the HTML files that are being loaded via Ajax and, therefore, not outlined in this chapter.

```
<div id="newContent"></div>  ◀••••••••••••••  <div id="content">
                                                  <div class="article">
                                                      <h3 data-title="Article 1">Article 1</h3>
                                                      <p class="by-line"><span data-author="Blanchard, Jay" cl
                                                      <p>Lorem ipsum dolor sit amet, consectetur adipiscing el
                                                      <a href="" class="mover">move to top</a> Tags:<span
                                                  </div>
                                                  <div class="article">
                                                      <h3 data-title="Article 2">Article 2</h3>
                                                      <p class="by-line"><span data-author="Castro, Jesse" cla
                                                      <p>Lorem ipsum dolor sit amet, consectetur adipiscing el
                                                      <a href="" class="mover">move to top</a> Tags:<span
                                                  </div>
                                                  <div class="article">
                                                      <h3 data-title="Article 3">Article 3</h3>
                                                      <p class="by-line"><span data-author="Awl, Dave" class="
                                                      <p>Lorem ipsum dolor sit amet, consectetur adipiscing el
                                                      <a href="" class="mover">move to top</a> Tags:<span
                                                  </div>
                                                  <div class="article">
                                                      <h3 data-title="Article 4">Article 4</h3>
                                                      <p class="by-line"><span data-author="Blanchard, Jay" cl
                                                      <p>Lorem ipsum dolor sit amet, consectetur adipiscing el
                                                      <a href="" class="mover">move to top</a> Tags:<span
```

D Take the **#content** from the remote page and place it into the **#newContent** on the calling page.

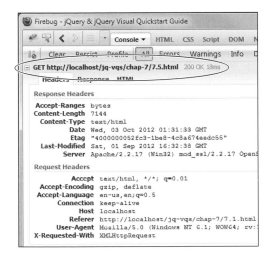

Looking at the console in Firebug, you'll see a line for each page that you loaded **E**. If there's an error loading the page, the line will be red and you'll see information concerning the error **F**.

continues on next page

E The HTTP request for the file was successfully made.

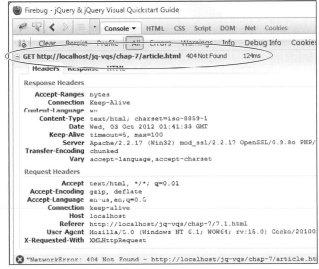

F The page you were looking for was not found.

Examine the console information more closely on a successful Ajax request in Firebug by expanding the line. You'll see that there are three tabs: one for the request and response headers ⓖ, another for the response ⓗ, and one for the HTML that's returned ⓘ.

Because you requested a full page using the **load()** command, the page's full markup is returned on a successful request, not just the element that you want to work with. The **load()** method processes the returned page when a filter is applied, as you did in the exercise, and places the filtered content into the proper element.

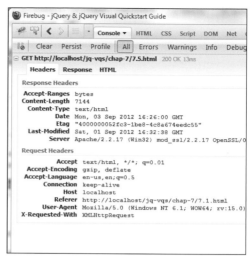

ⓖ The request and response headers tab.

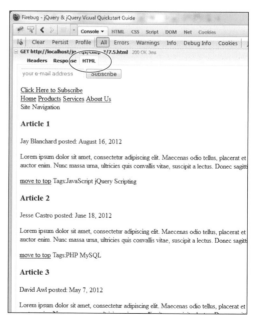

ⓗ The markup of the response.

ⓘ HTML returned from the request.

Managing Ajax loaded content

If you're a savvy developer (and I believe that you are!), you're probably a bit ahead of me at this point and you may have noticed something that you consider unusual. None of the jQuery functions work on any of the content that has been loaded into `index.html`!

The jQuery code that you include in a page is executed when the DOM has completely loaded into the page and attached event handlers to all the existing elements. When new information is loaded into the page, jQuery isn't aware of those elements and consequently none of the event handlers for those elements are attached.

Have no fear, though—there's a simple way to make sure that event handlers get properly attached to new content without requiring page refreshes or any special magic. Allow me to introduce the **on()** method.

The **on()** method lets you attach event handlers to any event that occurs within the document, regardless of when the element

needed for the event is added to the document. (You'll find an in-depth technical description of the **on()** method on jQuery's website at http://api.jquery.com/on/.) You use this method by attaching it to an element that you know exists when the page loads. You'll often see the **on()** method attached to the document or body like this:

$(document).on(..

$('body').on(..

The reason for attaching the **on()** method to an element you know will exist at the time the page initially loads is because of *event bubbling*.

When an event occurs, the information about the event bubbles up the DOM tree through each ancestor of the event target. By attaching the **on()** method to an element in the tree that exists when the page loads and that contains the event target, you can be assured that the event will bubble up to a location where it will be handled by your jQuery code ❶.

continues on next page

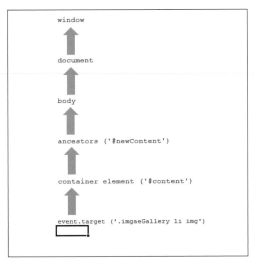

❶ An event bubbles up the DOM tree.

To see the effects of event bubbling and the **on()** method, you'll make some changes to your existing jQuery code. Because everything is being loaded into the **div** with **id="newContent"**, you'll bind **on()** to that selector.

To use the on() method to attach event handlers:

1. Locate the function that you created for the lightbox in **jquery.custom.js**. Comment out the first line of the function:

   ```
   //$('.imageGallery li img')
   .click(function() {
   ```

2. Set up a new line to be the first line of the function using the **on()** method. The syntax is simple: Select the proper **div**, and bind the **on()** method to it with the event as the first argument and the original selector as the second argument :

   ```
   $('#newContent').on('click',
   → '.imageGallery li img',
   → function() {
   ```

3. Upload the **jquery.custom.js** file to your web server and reload **index. html**. Click on the Gallery link in the floating menu and then click on one of the images. The lightbox is restored to operation 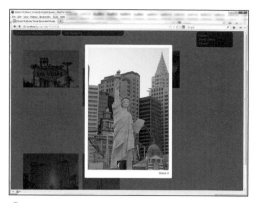.

You'll no doubt have noticed that a lot of the elements that you added with jQuery before are no longer there. These were added using some of jQuery's utility functions and were just for demonstration purposes.

K The lightbox is working again.

> **TIP** It's best to break up a hover event into its **mouseenter** and **mouseleave** parts when using the **on()** method.

You can now work your way through your **jquery.custom.js** file and change to the **on()** method where needed.

Now that you know how to get information from the server, let's turn our attention to sending information to the server using the **post()** method.

To use the post() method:

1. Open **index.html** in your text editor and make sure that the markup for the e-mail registration form is complete:

```
<form name="registration"
→ action="inc/php/registration.php"
→ method="post">

<input type="text" name=
→ "userEMail" placeholder="your
→ e-mail address" />

<button type="submit">

Subscribe</button>

</form>
```

2. Place the **index.html** file on your web server and open it in your web browser.

3. Update **jquery.custom.js** with a function to handle the e-mail form submission. Start by attaching the selector for the form to the **submit()** event handler. Be sure to prevent the default action of the submit button:

```
$('form[name="registration"]')

.submit(function(e) {

e.preventDefault();
```

4. Get information about where the form is to be processed and place it into a variable:

```
var formAction =
→ $(this).attr('action');
```

continues on next page

5. Place the form data into a variable by using the jQuery **serialize()** method:

```
var formData =
→ $(this).serialize();
```

The **serialize()** method takes all of the form input names as well as their values and places them into a key-value query string that can then be parsed by the server-side script. For this exercise the string might look like this:

```
userEmail=you@youremail.com
```

6. Create the **post()** function with the server-side script address as the first argument and the serialized form data as the second argument:

```
$.post(

    formAction,

    formData,
```

7. Set up the callback function for the **post()** method. The server is expected to send a response (the response is held in the variable called **data**) of **1** if the submission is successful:

```
function(data){

    if(1 == data) {
```

8. Clear the form and change the place-holder of the input element if the submission is successful :

```
$('form[name="registration"]
→ input')

.val('');

$('input[name="userEMail"]')

.attr('placeholder', 'Thank you!');
```

Ⓛ The e-mail address was successfully saved to the database.

Using PHP and MySQL

For exercises requiring server interaction, PHP has been used for the scripting language and MySQL has been used for the database. You are free to use any server-side technology you'd like.

All of the PHP scripts have been included in Appendix B and the downloadable code for the book. You'll also find the necessary scripts to set up your database to hold the information that's submitted.

Concepts for PHP and MySQL go beyond the scope of this book. Here are some good resources for learning about PHP and MySQL:

- *PHP and MySQL for Dynamic Web Sites: Visual QuickPro Guide, 4th Edition* by Larry Ullman (Peachpit Press)

- PHP documentation is available from the PHP website: http://www.php.net

- Information and documentation on MySQL is available from www.mysql.com/

M There must have been a problem with the submission of the e-mail address.

N Viewing the proper response from the server-side script in Firebug.

9. Handle an unsuccessful attempt by clearing the form and letting the user know that they need to resubmit their information. You do this by changing the placeholder **M**:

```
} else {
$('form[name="registration"]
 input')
.val('');
$('input[name="userEMail"]')
.attr('placeholder', 'Please
 resubmit!');
        }
    });
});
```

10. Upload **jquery.custom.js** to your web server. Provided your server-side scripts work properly, you should be able to submit e-mail addresses to your database and watch for the proper responses in your console tool **N**.

TIP Always develop and test your server-side scripts before applying any jQuery code. Trying to perform initial testing of server-side processes while also trying to implement jQuery code can and will make the troubleshooting process much more difficult.

Working with JSON

On many occasions, you'll want to work with a remote website to request data and then work with that response in your web pages. Many websites provide application programming interfaces (APIs) that accept your request and then send a response back to you.

In many cases, the data they provide is delivered to you in the form of JSON (JavaScript Object Notation), which is a lightweight data format used for describing information in a particular way. Typically, the data in JSON is defined in name-value pairs or arrays that can you can work with easily. (You can learn more about JSON at www.json.org.)

There is one problem, though. Ajax requests are typically blocked from going outside of your own domain to request or retrieve the data. There are some complex ways of getting around this, but fortunately with jQuery, you can request JSON with Padding—otherwise known as JSONP.

Because the "same origin policy" prohibits requests across domains by scripts in your pages, you'll need another method to retrieve the information simply and effectively. Essentially, you can *include* scripts, images, and other bits of information from other websites in your web pages. To make this work, you inject a set of script tags into the remote site. The source of that script tag is the URL for the remote server's API. The remote server, seeing that the script belongs to it, returns the requested data in the form of JSONP.

TIP You must always include a callback as part of the URL string for the API you're requesting.

To show you how this works, let's set up a request to Twitter and include some of your tweets in your web page.

To use getJSON():

1. Edit **index.html** (Script **7.6.html**) to include a container in your floating menu for the tweets:

```
<div class="sidebar">
<a href="7.5.html">
Articles</a><br />
<a href="7.4.html">Photo Gallery
</a><br />
<a href="7.3.html">Recipes
</a><br />
<hr />
<div id="tweets">Recent Tweets -
→ </div>
</div>
```

   The tweets will be part of your floating menu.

2. Save **index.html** and upload it to your web server.

3. Modify **jquery.custom.js** to include the function for retrieving the tweets. Start by specifying the URL. Be sure to replace **YOUR_USER_NAME** with your Twitter username:

```
var twitterURL = 'http://twitter.
→ com/statuses/user_timeline.
→ json?screen_name=YOUR_USER_
→ NAME&count=8&callback=?';
```

   In addition to your username, you specified the number of tweets to get.

   Note the **&callback=?** at the end of the URL string. You must include this to get data back from the API in the JSONP format.

continues on next page

4. Initiate the Ajax request for the JSON:

```
$.getJSON(twitterURL,
→ function(data){
```

5. Perform a loop through the returned JSON data so that you can parse it properly. Because each portion of the Twitter response is part of a JSON object, you can address it by its name, as in **item.text**:

```
$.each(data, function(i, item){

var tweetText = item.text;
```

6. While looping through each item, use regular expressions to make sure links in tweets are captured and formatted properly:

```
tweetText = tweetText.replace
→ (/http:\/\/\S+/g, '<a href="$&"
→ target="blank">$&</a>');

tweetText = tweetText.replace(/(@)
→ (\w+)/g, '<a href="http://twitter.
→ com/$2" target="blank">$1$2
→ </a> ');

tweetText = tweetText.replace
→ (/(#)(\w+)/g, '<a href="http://
→ search.twitter.com/search?q=
→ %23$2" target="blank">$1$2
→ </a> ');
```

7. Append each tweet to the tweet container:

```
$('#tweets')

.append('<div class="tweet">'+
→ tweetText +'</div>');

    });

});
```

8. Save and place **jquery.custom.js** on your web server. Reload **index.html** and your tweets will show up in the floating menu .

A Tweet, tweet, tweet! A little birdy has dropped some information into your web page.

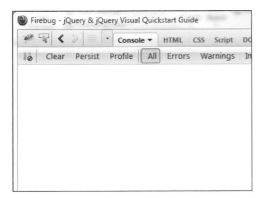

B The console tab doesn't have your JSON request.

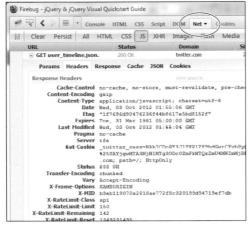

C The Net tab contains the request and response information for the JSON information.

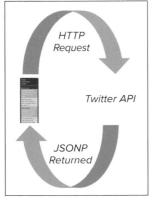

D The request-response cycle is illustrated for the Ajax function.

Before you head off to Firebug to view the request and response, be prepared for a little surprise. The request and response do not appear under the Console tab like other Ajax requests **B**.

Remember that you are actually *including* information from another website because you used a set of script tags referencing that site. In Firebug you can see request and response headers by looking under the Net tab **C**.

When the menu loads into the page, you're generating an HTTP request to the Twitter API via the URL that you included in the function to get the tweets. If the request is successful, the Twitter API returns the JSONP data, which is then parsed and placed into the page **D**.

Using jQuery's Ajax shorthand methods will get you started down the path of including dynamic content quickly in your websites, but there is a lot more that you can learn. Follow up by reading the documentation on the low-level jQuery **ajax()** method on the jQuery website at http://api.jquery.com/jQuery.ajax/.

It's now time to take a closer look at some methods that you can use to give your websites some cool visual effects. The jQuery animation methods are up next!

Rewind and Review

Take a few moments to reflect on what you've learned in this chapter:

- What one application must you always use to test your Ajax functions?

- Which event binding method should you use when content loaded via Ajax doesn't respond to jQuery events normally?

- When you're troubleshooting Ajax issues, what is the one tool you should have in your toolbox?

- Should you use **on()** with the jQuery **hover()** method?

- What does the acronym JSON stand for? How is JSON formed?

- What is event bubbling?

- The same origin policy prevents you from performing what specific action?

- What does a callback in the URL query string signify?

Creating Captivating Effects

There may be nothing more exciting than easily adding animations to your websites and web applications. Whether subtle or bold, well-done animations can be attention-grabbing and add a wow factor that will keep your website visitors coming back time and time again.

The jQuery library provides a number of animation and effects methods that allow you to fade and move elements at will. Adding the jQuery UI library will also allow you to transition between colors and even classes. To complete the effects library you can use the jQuery easing plugin, which allows you to control the animation speed at different points during the animation sequence.

The combination of the jQuery library and the plugins gives you a wide range of options for adding fun and useful effects to your websites. Let's get started!

Controlling Visibility

Catching the attention of your website visitors is a piece of cake when using the jQuery effects methods. These methods are divided into three distinct groups: controlling an item's visibility, making items move, and then combining effects to create custom animations.

Let's focus first on controlling an item's visibility (see **Table 8.1**).

Let's give the user the option of hiding or showing the recent tweets that were added to the floating menu.

To use the toggle() method:

1. Modify the floating menu in your **index.html** file (Script **8.1.html**) to add a span to the title "Recent Tweets," as highlighted here:

   ```
   <div id="tweets" class="shown">
   Recent Tweets <span>(hide)
   → </span></div>
   ```

   You'll also need to add a class to the element. That will be used to determine what text to display in the span.

2. Save the file and upload it to your web server. You'll see the span, and the tweets are displayed .

3. Compose a new function to hide or show the tweets in **jquery.custom.js**. Start by binding the click event handler:

   ```
   $('#tweets').click(function() {
   ```

TABLE 8.1 jQuery Visibility Methods

Function Name	Use It To...
fadeIn()	Display the selected elements by fading them to opaque.
fadeOut()	Hide the selected elements by fading them to transparent.
fadeTo()	Adjust the degree of opacity of the selected elements.
fadeToggle()	Show or hide the selected elements by animating their opacity.
hide()	Instantly hide the selected elements.
show()	Immediately display the selected elements.
toggle()	Show or hide the selected elements using the same event handler.

Ⓐ The span indicating you can hide the tweets is shown.

B The tweets are hidden, but you can click to show them again.

C The elements collapse or expand depending on which side of the toggle is triggered. Here the animation is captured at its midpoint.

4. Bind the toggle method to the elements having a class of **tweet**:

   ```
   $('.tweet').toggle('slow');
   ```

   At this point you could close out the function and the elements would either be hidden or shown on each click. To make sure the visitor knows what's going on, let's add a little more to the function.

5. Add a conditional statement to test to see if **#tweets** has the class **shown**:

   ```
   if(true == $(this).
   hasClass('shown')) {
   ```

6. Remove the class if it exists and set the span text to indicate that the visitor can click again to show the tweets **B**:

   ```
   $(this).removeClass('shown')
   .find('span').text('(show)');
   ```

7. Add the class **shown** if it doesn't exist and change the span text back to its original wording. Close out the function's brackets:

   ```
   } else {
       $(this).addClass('shown')
       .find('span').text('(hide)');
   }
   });
   ```

8. Save **jquery.custom.js** and upload it to your web server. Click the "Recent Tweets" text and you'll see your tweets fold and unfold **C**.

The **toggle()** function is essentially two functions: **hide()** and **show()**. The function relies on the state of the object's visibility to determine which action it should take when it's triggered. You could construct this same function using **hide()** and

continues on next page

`show()` separately, but using the `toggle()` method makes your function much tidier.

For added effect you can also introduce an easing function. It's as simple as including the easing plugin and then placing the easing function of your choice in the call to the `toggle()` method.

To use the easing plugin:

1. Download the easing plugin from http://gsgd.co.uk/sandbox/jquery/easing/ and save it to the `inc/jquery/` folder on your web server.

2. Modify `index.html` (Script `8.2.html`) to include the easing file. Place the reference to the easing plugin after the line where you add the jQuery core file:

   ```
   <script src="inc/jquery/
   ↪jquery-1.7.2.js"></script>

   <script src="inc/jquery/
   ↪jquery.custom.js"></script>

   <script src="inc/jquery/
   ↪jquery.easing.1.3.js"></script>
   ```

3. Save the `index.html` file and upload it to your web server.

4. Open the `jquery.custom.js` file in your text editor and add the easing method call to the toggle function you just created:

   ```
   $('.tweet')

   .toggle('slow', 'easeInSine');
   ```

5. Upload the modified `jquery.custom.js` file to your web server and load `index.html` into your browser. Click on the "Recent Tweets" title to see the effect.

Now is a good time for a little experimentation. Try changing the duration of the toggle function and changing the easing method to see the various effects available.

Easing Animations

What, exactly, is easing? The simplest explanation is that easing controls the speed of an animation during specific points in time while the animation is running.

For instance, if you want an animation to start slowly but end more quickly, you might choose **easeInQuad**. How about adding a little bounce to the end of the animation? Use **easeOutBounce**.

Easing works by changing a CSS property at specific points in time during the animation. Each easing function has a mathematical definition that determines when the CSS property is changed. The jQuery easing plugin (available for download from http://gsgd.co.uk/sandbox/jquery/easing/) defines a number of easing functions to enhance your animations with.

For a visual representation of how the various easing functions work, James Padolsey has provided an online widget: http://james.padolsey.com/demos/jquery/easing/.

TIP Depending on the elements being animated, some easing methods will work and look better. The key to using easing effectively is knowing what's available and experimenting to find the right easing method for the elements that you're working with.

TABLE 8.2 jQuery Motion Methods

Function Name	Use It To...
slideDown()	Display the selected elements by animating the height of the element from top to bottom.
slideToggle()	Show or hide the selected elements with a sliding motion.
slideUp()	Hide the selected elements by animating the height of the element from bottom to top.

Ⓐ The version information is displayed on the site.

Managing Motion

The bulk of jQuery's motion effects are handled by custom animation methods, but there are a couple of specific methods that you can use to give motion to selected elements (see **Table 8.2**).

The sliding effects work by animating the height, either from the top or the bottom depending on the method. The **slideUp()** method animates the height upward. The reverse is true for the **slideDown()** method. You can manipulate the duration and add easing to the methods to change the look of the animation.

To use the slideToggle() method:

1. Add a new element to **index.html** (Script **8.3.html**) to define a version number Ⓐ.

   ```
   <div id="version">
   <a href="">Version</a>
   <div class="version_info">
     Version 0.6 Beta
   </div></div>
   ```

   The new element should be placed just before the opening **div** tag with a class of **pageWrapper**.

2. Save the file and upload it to your web server.

continues on next page

3. Create a new function to toggle the version information in your **jquery.custom.js** file. Start by binding the link to the click method:

```
$('#version a')
.click(function(e){
e.preventDefault();
```

4. Define the function to apply **slideToggle()** to the proper **div**:

```
$(this).parent()
.find('.version_info')
.slideToggle();
});
```

5. Upload the jQuery file to your web server and load the page into your browser. Click on the Version link to hide or show the version information .

B The information slides up and out of site!

TABLE 8.3 jQuery Custom Animation Methods

Function Name	Use It To
animate()	Perform a custom animation of a set of CSS properties on the selected elements.
clearQueue()	Empty the queue of all of the queued functions that have not yet been run.
dequeue()	Execute the next function on the stack of queued functions for the selected elements.
delay()	Set a timer to delay execution of subsequent functions in the queue.
queue()	Show the queue of functions to be executed on the selected elements.
stop()	Stop the currently running animation on the selected elements.

Composing Custom Animations

The bread and butter of jQuery's effect methods lies in its capability to create custom animations by manipulating several CSS properties all at the same time. This provides you with limitless possibilities when constructing effects. In addition to the effects themselves, jQuery provides several methods for managing those effects (see **Table 8.3**).

In order to demonstrate animation, you'll go back to the article page and replace the movement function. The new function that you'll create to perform the animation is the most complex of the functions in this book and requires the creation of a new method where you extend the functionality of jQuery.

The basic premise for this function is to be able to animate the selected article to the top of the list while moving only the articles above the selected article down to make room for the change. You've got to plan well before creating a complex interaction like this one. Be sure to sketch out your ideas before you start to code.

continues on next page

Let's start by creating the helper function, `outerHTML()`.

To create the outerHTML() helper function:

1. Open **jquery.custom.js** in your text editor and declare a new jQuery function called **outerHTML**:

   ```
   $.fn.outerHTML = function() {
   ```

2. Create the object that you want returned from the function. Then close out the function:

   ```
   return $(this).clone()
   .wrap('<div></div>').parent().
   → html();
   };
   ```

   In this case you'll want to return a clone of the object that you bind to it. The clone's parent HTML will be wrapped in **div** tags. The reason that you want to clone the element is so that the original is not modified.

3. Save the **jquery.custom.js** file.

Adding a function to jQuery is as easy as using the **fn** method. You start the function as you normally would, with the **$**, and then you call the **fn** method followed by your new function name:

$.fn.functionName

At that point, your function can be as simple or as complex as you'd like it to be. Just be sure to return an object so that your function can be chained with other jQuery methods.

Before you add the new mover method, you'll need to comment out the function you previously created by placing **/*** at the beginning of the code block and ***/** at the end of the block Ⓐ.

```
/* article mover */
/*$('#newContent').on('click', '.mover', function(e) {
    $('.mover').click(function(e) {
    e.preventDefault();
    $('#content div:first').before($(this).parent('div'));
    $(this).parent('div').insertBefore($('#content div:first'));
});*/
```

Ⓐ The old mover function has been commented out so it doesn't interfere with the new function.

To use the animate() method:

1. Add an ID to each article in **article.html** (Script **8.4.html** is a simplified version of the article page):

```
<div class="article"
→ id="article1">
<h3>Article 1</h3>
<p>Lorem ipsum dolor sit amet...
→ </p>
<a href="" class="mover">
move to top</a></div>
<div class="article"
→ id="article2">
<h3>Article 2</h3>
<p>Lorem ipsum dolor sit amet...
→ </p>
<a href="" class="mover">
move to top</a></div>
<div class="article"
→ id="article3">
<h3>Article 3</h3>
<p>Lorem ipsum dolor sit amet...
→ </p>
<a href="" class="mover">
move to top</a></div>
<div class="article"
→ id="article4">
<h3>Article 4</h3>
<p>Lorem ipsum dolor sit amet...
→ </p>
<a href="" class="mover">
move to top</a></div>
<div class="article"
→ id="article5">
<h3>Article 5</h3>
<p>Lorem ipsum dolor sit amet...
→ </p>
<a href="" class="mover">
move to top</a></div>
```

2. Save **article.html** and place it on your web server **B**.

continues on next page

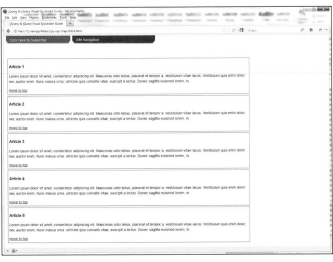

B The scaled-down article page is ready for animation.

3. Start the new mover function in **jquery.custom.js** by using the **on()** method to bind click functions to the mover links in the content **div**:

```
$('#content')
.on('click', '.mover', function(e) {
e.preventDefault();
```

4. Declare a group of variables that will be used in the mover function. The variables are all objects based on selectors along with jQuery methods to get the height and position of elements:

```
var article = $(this).parent();

var contentHeight =
→ $('#content').innerHeight();

var articleHeight =
→ article.height();

var articleTop =
→ article.position().top;

var moveUp = articleTop;

var moveDown = articleHeight;

var articleID =
→ article.attr("id");

var articleHTML =
→ article.outerHTML();
```

The last variable that you'll declare uses the helper function you created in the previous exercise. It returns the cloned article **div**.

5. Create the function that tests for the articles needing to be moved down. You'll only be moving down the articles above the selected article. To find out which ones you have to move, you loop through each article and return false when you get to the article you've selected to move to the top.

```
$('.article').each(function() {
if ($(this).attr("id") ==
→ articleID)
    return false;
}
```

6. Animate each of the articles above the selected article down, changing their CSS top value by a factor of one article's height, which is contained in the variable **moveDown**. The animation takes 1000 milliseconds to complete, as defined at the end of the **animate()** method:

```
$(this).animate({
    "top": '+=' + moveDown
    }, 1000);
});
```

Because you looped through each article before encountering the article to be moved, **$(this)** is an object that contains the articles above the selected article. Now it's time to move the selected article up to the top of the list and perform some cleanup.

continues on next page

7. Use the **animate()** method to move the selected article to the top of the container **div**:

```
article.animate({
    "top": '-=' + moveUp
}, 1000, function() {
```

The article is moved up by the amount contained in the variable **moveUp**, which is the top value of the article's CSS position in relation to the content container.

8. Remove the old article, because you'll be replacing it with the cloned article to ensure that everything is in the right order in the DOM after the animation **C**:

```
article.remove();
```

Without cloning, the element would still move in the web browser for the user. In the DOM, the article is still in the same place that it started. Another click on an article might lead to some funny animation and a very disordered page. You'll add the cloned element to the beginning of the markup after you've removed the clone's old twin.

```
⊟ <div id="content">
    ⊞ <div id="article3" class="article" style="">
    ⊞ <div id="article1" class="article" style="">
    ⊞ <div id="article2" class="article" style="">
    ⊞ <div id="article4" class="article" style="">
    ⊞ <div id="article5" class="article" style="">
  </div>
```

C The markup in the DOM after the move has been made. Note that article 3 is now in the top position.

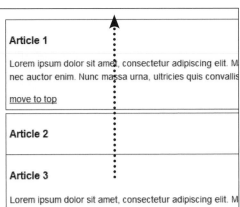

D The article in mid-animation to the top of the list.

9. Get the markup that's currently in the content container. Then replace the markup with the cloned element plus the current elements:

```
var oldHTML =
→ $('#content').html();

$('#content')

.html(articleHTML + oldHTML);
```

10. Remove any style tags that would have been applied to the articles during the move to keep things clean. Then close up your brackets:

```
        $('.article').attr('style', '');

        });

});
```

11. Save the **jquery.custom.js** file and place it on your web server in the proper location.

12. Load **article.html** into your browser and click on any of the "move to top" links. The selected article should transition to the top of the list while those originally above it should slide down **D**.

That's one cool effect, and you've seen that the animation was easier to implement than the math involved in calculating how much to move the elements. Keep in mind that you can also animate other CSS properties that have numerical values—you're not just limited to position.

As fun as animating elements is, it isn't the end of your journey to becoming proficient with jQuery. Next you'll learn how to use some of jQuery's utility methods.

Rewind and Review

Take a few moments to reflect on what you've learned in this chapter:

- What CSS property are you animating when you use one of the slide methods?

- How do you use easing to make animations more interesting?

- Which library must you use to animate color?

- What method is required to create a function in jQuery?

- Where should you include the easing plugin reference?

- What two functions does the toggle method use?

Turning on jQuery's Utilities

The jQuery library provides a number of handy functions known as *utilities* (http://api.jquery.com/category/utilities/). These utility functions don't have the glamour associated with all the other functionality that jQuery provides, but these powerful little tools will enhance the jQuery code that you write and use every day.

Many of these utilities mimic their pure JavaScript counterparts but come with the ease of use that the jQuery library supplies. The jQuery library also provides some specialized utility functions to store and remove data elements on DOM elements or loop through a selected set of elements. You'll also find methods to use when parsing XML or JSON when the need arises.

Numerous utility methods are available (see **Table 9.1** on the next page). The focus here will be on the utilities that you're likely to use most in your day-to-day coding, so let's get started!

TABLE 9.1 jQuery Utility Methods

Function Name	Use It To...
`clearQueue()`	Remove all items from the queue that haven't been run yet.
`jQuery.contains()`	Check to see if a DOM element is within another DOM element.
`jQuery.data()`	Store arbitrary data associated with a specified element.
`dequeue()`	Execute the next function on the queue for the selected elements. Takes the name of a queue as an argument.
`jQuery.dequeue()`	Execute the next function on the queue for the matched selected elements. Takes a DOM element and the name of a queue as arguments.
`jQuery.each()`	Iterate over objects and arrays.
`jQuery.extend()`	Merge the contents of two or more objects together into the first object.
`jQuery.globalEval()`	Execute some JavaScript code globally.
`jQuery.grep()`	Find the elements of an array that satisfy a filter function.
`jQuery.inArray()`	Search for a specified value within an array and return its index (or −1 if not found).
`jQuery.isArray()`	Determine if an argument is an array.
`jQuery.isEmptyObject()`	Check to see if an object is empty (contains no properties).
`jQuery.isFunction()`	Determine if the argument passed to it is a JavaScript function object.
`jQuery.isNumeric()`	Determine whether its argument is a number.
`jQuery.isPlainObject()`	Check to see if an object is a plain object (created using "{}" or "new Object").
`jQuery.isWindow()`	Determine if its argument is a window.
`jQuery.isXMLDoc()`	Check to see if a DOM node is within an XML document or is an XML document.
`jQuery.makeArray()`	Convert an array-like object into a true JavaScript array.
`jQuery.map()`	Translate all items in an array or object to a new array of items.
`jQuery.merge()`	Merge the contents of two arrays together into the first array.
`jQuery.noop()`	This is an empty function.
`jQuery.now()`	Return a number representing the current time.
`jQuery.parseJSON()`	Return the resulting JavaScript object from a well-formed JSON string.
`jQuery.parseXML()`	Parse a string into an XML document.
`jQuery.proxy()`	Take a function and return a new function that will have a particular context.
`jQuery.queue()`	Show the queue of functions to be executed on the selected element.
`jQuery.removeData()`	Remove a previously stored piece of data.
`jQuery.support`	Determine the presence of different browser features.
`jQuery.trim()`	Remove the whitespace from the beginning and end of a string.
`jQuery.type()`	Determine the internal JavaScript Class of an object.
`jQuery.unique()`	Sort an array of DOM elements, in place, with the duplicates removed. This only works on arrays of DOM elements, not strings or numbers.

Looping Through Elements

There will be times when you want to loop through a set of objects and apply a function to them. The jQuery library provides a great utility for doing this: the **jQuery.each()** method.

To demonstrate, let's look at a table of products shipped and determine on which days certain numbers of items were shipped.

To use the jQuery.each() utility:

1. Open the **products.html** page created earlier (Script **9.1.html**) and modify the table cells for each column to add the class **"units"**. The markup here covers only a portion of the table as an example.

```
<tr>
    <td>2002-03-01</td>
    <td class="units">270</td>
    <td class="units">352</td>
    <td class="units">368</td>
    <td class="units">360</td>
    <td class="units">1350</td>
</tr>
<tr>
    <td>2002-03-02</td>
    <td class="units">250</td>
    <td class="units">212</td>
    <td class="units">374</td>
    <td class="units">310</td>
    <td class="units">1146</td>
</tr>
```

continues on next page

2. Place the following markup in the page just above the opening table tag:

```
Daily Units Shipped
<a href="100" class="dailySales">
100+</a> |
<a href="200" class="dailySales">
200+</a> |
<a href="300" class="dailySales">
300+</a> |
<a href="400" class="dailySales">
400+</a> |
<a href="500" class="dailySales">
500+</a><br />
```

3. Save the products page and upload it to your web server **Ⓐ**.

4. Edit the **jquery.custom.js** file and start a function by binding a click event handler to the **dailySales** class:

```
$('.dailySales').click(function(e){
```

5. Remove the **numberClass** highlight from any table cell that might have it. Then prevent the default behavior of the clicked link:

```
$('td')
.removeClass('numberHighlight');
e.preventDefault();
```

6. Save the actual integer value of the clicked link's **href** attribute in a variable. You'll be using JavaScript's **parseInt()** function to turn text into a number:

```
var thisValue = parseInt($(this).
  attr('href'));
```

Text into a number? As far as you may be concerned, the item on your screen looks like a number, but it really isn't. It is text that represents a number because HTML passes around strings, not numbers.

JavaScript, and therefore jQuery, has several classifications of data types. Some things are text, some are numbers, and yet others are objects. To perform the calculation needed for this function, you'll have to change the text string into a number that can be manipulated with math.

7. Create a set of table cell objects with a class of *units* that are not the last cell in each row, because you don't want to include daily totals:

```
var units = $('.units')
.not(':last-child');
```

Products

Daily Units Shipped <u>100+</u> | <u>200+</u> | <u>300+</u> | <u>400+</u> | <u>500+</u>

Date	Water Pistols	Balloons	Party Packs	Streamers	Total Shipped Today
2002-03-01	270	352	368	360	1350
2002-03-02	250	212	374	310	1146
2002-03-03	167	208	421	311	1107
2002-03-04	165	223	404	297	1089
2002-03-05	115	214	409	301	1039
Total By Items	967	1209	1976	1279	

Ⓐ The products table with the new set of links for selecting Daily Units Shipped.

8. Use the **jQuery.each()** utility to start the loop through each object, get its text, and change that text to an integer, and then save the value to a variable:

```
jQuery.each(units, function() {
var cellValue =
 parseInt($(this).html());
```

9. During the iteration, test the current table cell's value against the value gained from the clicked link. If the test is true, apply a class to the current table cell. Then close out the brackets to end the loop and the event handler:

```
if(cellValue > thisValue){
    $(this).addClass
 ('numberHighlight');
}
});
});
```

10. Save the **jquery.custom.js** file and place it on your web server. Reload the products page into your web browser and click on one of the links **B**.

Now that you know how to iterate over a set of objects, let's add some more functionality by storing a little data in the page and displaying that data when needed.

TIP Don't confuse the **jQuery.each()** method with the **$(element).each()** traversal method. Although their operation is nearly the same, the traversal method is designed to work exclusively with jQuery objects. The **jQuery.each()** method can loop through objects, such as those created in **JSON** or a collection of elements, as well as arrays.

TIP Letter case is important when using the utility methods. Be sure to start utilities with "jQuery," not "jquery."

Products

Daily Units Shipped 100+ | 200+ | 300+ | 400+ | 500+

Date	Water Pistols	Balloons	Party Packs	Streamers	Total Shipped Today
2002-03-01	270	352	368	360	1350
2002-03-02	250	212	374	310	1146
2002-03-03	167	208	421	311	1107
2002-03-04	165	223	404	297	1089
2002-03-05	115	214	409	301	1039
Total By Items	967	1209	1976	1279	

B Party packs are consistently shipping more than 300 units per day.

Setting and Getting Data

There's hardly a website today that doesn't use stored data to produce dynamic results when the website visitor calls for it. Within the jQuery utility functions is a method that you can use to attach data to DOM elements for later retrieval. Simply enough, it's called the **jQuery.data()** method.

To learn how this works, you'll total the numbers in the last column of the products table when the page loads and then store the final result as data attached to the table **Ⓐ**. You'll retrieve that data for display when the user asks for it by clicking a link.

To use the jQuery.data() method to store data on a DOM element:

1. Start by creating a function in **jquery. custom.js** that will total the values of each shipped item:

   ```
   function getPeriodTotal() {
   ```

2. Declare a variable that will ultimately hold the sum of the shipped column:

   ```
   var periodTotal = 0;
   ```

3. Get the objects that need to be totaled and place them into a variable:

   ```
   var dailyShippedTotal =
   → $('.units').filter(':last-child');
   ```

```
<table id="product_table">  ◁──  'tableTotal', thisPeriod
    <thead >
     <tr>
      <th>Date</th>
      <th>Water Pistols</th>
      <th>Balloons</th>
      <th>Party Packs</th>
      <th>Streamers</th>
      <th>Total Shipped Today</th>
     </tr>
    </thead>
    <tbody >
     <tr>
```

Ⓐ You'll attach a bit of data to the table.

4. Create a loop using the **jQuery.each()** method to get the value of each object and add them together:

```
jQuery.each(dailyShippedTotal,
→ function(){
      periodTotal = periodTotal +
      → parseInt($(this).html());
});
```

5. Return the calculated number from the function and close out the function:

```
return periodTotal;

}
```

6. Retrieve the totaled column by calling the function and assigning the returned value to a variable:

```
var thisPeriod = getPeriodTotal();
```

7. Attach the total to the table element using the **jQuery.data()** method by assigning it to the table with a key (**tableTotal**):

```
var productTable =

$('#products_table');

jQuery.data(productTable,
→ 'tableTotal', thisPeriod);
```

When retrieving the total for the table, you'll use the key that you assigned to get the data. Let's set that up now.

To use the jQuery.data() method to get stored data values:

1. Open **products.html** (Script **9.2.html**) in your text editor and add the following markup just above the table tag:

   ```
   <a href="totalShipped">
   Total Units Shipped</a>
   (this period)<br />
   ```

2. Save **products.html** and upload it to your web server. Load the page into your browser **B**.

3. Add a click handler to **jquery.custom.js** for the link that you placed into the products page:

   ```
   $('a[href="totalShipped"]')
   .click(function(e){
   e.preventDefault();
   ```

4. Retrieve the information that was stored previously using **jQuery.data()** and place it into a variable:

   ```
   var theShippedTotal = jQuery.
   → data(productTable, 'tableTotal');
   ```

5. Locate the last table cell of the last row of the table and set its text to be the value of the variable **theShippedTotal**. Add a class to highlight the number when it appears and close out the click handler:

   ```
   $('tr').eq(6).find('td')
   .filter(':last-child')
   .text(theShippedTotal)
   .addClass('numberHighlight');
   });
   ```

Products

Daily Units Shipped <u>100+</u> | <u>200+</u> | <u>300+</u> | <u>400+</u> | <u>500+</u>
<u>Total Units Shipped</u> (this period)

Date	Water Pistols	Balloons	Party Packs	Streamers	Total Shipped Today
2002-03-01	270	352	368	360	1350
2002-03-02	250	212	374	310	1146
2002-03-03	167	208	421	311	1107
2002-03-04	165	223	404	297	1089
2002-03-05	115	214	409	301	1039
Total By Items	967	1209	1976	1279	

B The link that you'll click to retrieve and show the stored data.

Products

Daily Units Shipped 100+ | 200+ | 300+ | 400+ | 500+
Total Units Shipped (this period)

Date	Water Pistols	Balloons	Party Packs	Streamers	Total Shipped Today
2002-03-01	270	352	368	360	1350
2002-03-02	250	212	374	310	1146
2002-03-03	167	208	421	311	1107
2002-03-04	165	223	404	297	1089
2002-03-05	115	214	409	301	1039
Total By Items	967	1209	1976	1279	5731

C The stored result is revealed.

6. Upload the jQuery file to your web server and reload the products page in your browser. Click the "Total Units Shipped" link and the stored number appears in the last table cell **C**.

These exercises were done using the jQuery library's low-level data utility, but jQuery also makes a high-level data method available that you can use to perform the same actions with a selector-based method. The syntax to set data using that method looks like this:

```
$('#production_table')
.data('tableTotal', thisPeriod);
```

Similarly, the syntax to get data using the higher-level method looks like this:

```
$('#production_table')
.data('tableTotal');
```

With the advent of HTML5 and its custom data attributes, the jQuery library has been adapted to have the ability to retrieve those values using the **data()** method. Given this tag:

```
<span data-camera="Canon">
```

you can use the **data()** method to recall the value with this jQuery code:

```
$('span').data('camera');
```

You can store multiple pieces of information on the same DOM element, including JSON style object definitions. Quite a powerful utility.

Rewind and Review

Take a few moments to reflect on what you've learned in this chapter:

- What types of items can you use **jQuery.each()** to iterate through?

- Is there a limit on the number of pieces of information you can attach to any single DOM element?

- What is the difference between the low-level **jQuery.data()** method and the high-level **data()** method?

- Can you parse JSON with a jQuery utility method?

- How do you use the **jQuery.data()** method with HTML5's custom data attributes?

10

Using Plugins

When jQuery was first introduced and found to be extendable, developers all over the world began developing their own libraries to take advantage of the features offered by the jQuery library. Many developers made their extensions to the jQuery library available to others and ultimately the extensions became known as plugins.

It seems that hardly a day goes by without a new jQuery plugin being introduced to the public. Developers have created plugins for displaying and manipulating images, handling form validation, performing complex animations, and much more. The choices are nearly endless, and there is typically more than one plugin that will solve a problem for you or enhance your website in some other way. You installed the easing plugin earlier to enhance your animations.

Once you've practiced jQuery for a while, you'll no doubt author plugins of your own. Perhaps you'll even share them with your fellow developers. Your education on plugins begins with learning how to use them, so it's time to get started.

In This Chapter

Working with Plugins

The first step in using a plugin is deciding what problem you're trying to solve or what kind of effect you'd like to add to your website. The second step is finding a group of plugins that fit and then choosing which one you'd like to use. The second step is usually the hardest.

TIP When choosing whether to use a jQuery plugin, you'll want to ask yourself if you can create something on your own that will solve your problem more quickly and easily.

When looking for a plugin, you should take a couple of key things into account. First, is it easy to use? Second, does it provide the kinds of options that you're looking for? Are the plugin and its options documented well enough to make customizing easy?

Let's look at a way to turn a boring list of images into an engaging scrolling carousel. One of the simplest-to-use plugins with plenty of options is jCarousel Lite. The download and documentation are available from www.gmarwaha.com/jquery/jcarousellite/.

To install jCarousel Lite:

1. Go to the website and click on the Download link. You'll be presented with a number of options **A**.

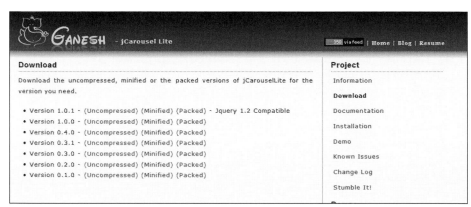

A The list of download options.

2. Click on the Uncompressed link for the latest version of the plugin. For this exercise we chose Version 1.0.1. You'll be presented with the JavaScript page **B**.

3. Save the file to your `inc/jquery/` directory.

4. Create a new HTML5 template that includes the navigation elements (Script **10.1.html**), CSS link, and the jQuery files previously used and save it as **carousel.html**.

5. Add a script tag to include the newly downloaded plugin **C**.

The script for the plugin is now installed and ready to go.

```
/**
 * jCarouselLite - jQuery plugin to navigate images/any content in a carousel style widget.
 * @requires jQuery v1.2 or above
 *
 * http://gmarwaha.com/jquery/jcarousellite/
 *
 * Copyright (c) 2007 Ganeshji Marwaha (gmarwaha.com)
 * Dual licensed under the MIT and GPL licenses:
 * http://www.opensource.org/licenses/mit-license.php
 * http://www.gnu.org/licenses/gpl.html
 *
 * Version: 1.0.1
 * Note: Requires jquery 1.2 or above from version 1.0.1
 */

/**
 * Creates a carousel-style navigation widget for images/any-content from a simple HTML markup.
 *
 * The HTML markup that is used to build the carousel can be as simple as...
 *
 *    <div class="carousel">
 *        <ul>
 *            <li><img src="image/1.jpg" alt="1"></li>
 *            <li><img src="image/2.jpg" alt="2"></li>
 *            <li><img src="image/3.jpg" alt="3"></li>
 *        </ul>
 *    </div>
 *
 * As you can see, this snippet is nothing but a simple div containing an unordered list of images.
 * You don't need any special "class" attribute, or a special "css" file for this plugin.
 * I am using a class attribute just for the sake of explanation here.
```

B The raw, uncompressed code for jCarousel Lite.

```
<!-- JAVASCRIPT / JQUERY -->
<!--[if lt IE 9]>
    <script src="http://html5shim.googlecode.com/svn/trunk/html5.js"></script>
<![endif]-->
<script src="inc/jquery/jquery-1.7.2.js"></script>
<script src="inc/jquery/jcarousellite_1.0.1.js"></script>    ◀••••••••••••
<script src="inc/jquery/jquery.easing.1.3.js"></script>
<script src="inc/jquery/jquery.custom.js"></script>
```

C Place the carousel's script tag after the jQuery core file.

To use jCarousel Lite:

1. Place the following markup in the **carousel.html** file (Script **10.2.html**). It's a simple unordered list within a set of **div** tags that has been given the class **jCarouselLite**:

```
<div class="jCarouselLite">

<ul>

<li><img src="images/thumb_
→ vegas01.jpg" width="250"></li>

<li><img src="images/thumb_
→ vegas02.jpg" width="250"></li>

<li><img src="images/thumb_
→ vegas03.jpg" width="250"></li>

<li><img src="images/thumb_
→ vegas04.jpg" width="250"></li>

<li><img src="images/thumb_
→ vegas05.jpg" width="250"></li>

<li><img src="images/thumb_
→ vegas06.jpg" width="250"></li>

<li><img src="images/thumb_
→ vegas07.jpg" width="250"></li>

<li><img src="images/thumb_
→ vegas08.jpg" width="250"></li>

<li><img src="images/thumb_
→ vegas09.jpg" width="250"></li>

<li><img src="images/thumb_
→ vegas10.jpg" width="250"></li>

<li><img src="images/thumb_
→ vegas11.jpg" width="250"></li>

</ul>

</div>
```

2. Save **carousel.html** and upload it to your web server. Load the page into your browser to see the images in a list **D**.

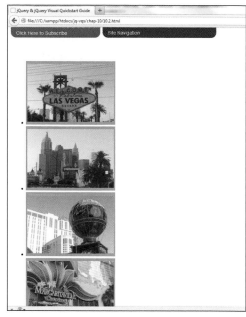

D The image list is ready to become something special.

E The carousel is up and running.

3. Open **jquery.custom.js** in your text editor and start the carousel function by selecting the **div**'s class and attaching the **jcarousellite()** method:

   `$(".jCarouselLite").jCarouselLite({`

4. Define the options to add easing, the speed of the carousel, and an automatic scrolling function. Then close out the method:

   ```
   easing: "easeOutSine",
   speed: 1000,
   auto: 1000
   });
   ```

5. Save the jQuery file, and then place it in the proper directory on your web server.

6. Reload **carousel.html** in your browser, and the carousel will have gained all of its CSS properties and will start scrolling **E**.

The jCarousel Lite plugin has all of the advantages that you'll want to seek out when searching for plugins because it's easy to use, has plenty of options, and is well documented.

Creating Your Own Plugins

Properly teaching you how to create jQuery plugins is a topic that's fairly extensive and beyond the scope of this book. But here's some information that will get you headed in the right direction.

Get started by reading the plugins tutorials on the jQuery website: http://docs.jquery.com/Plug-ins/Authoring.

As you begin to study and understand plugin authoring, continue to learn by examining the source code of the plugins that you use, like those included here.

Once you're on steady ground with all of the concepts, you can advance your understanding and skills by reading Addy Osmani's excellent blog post on taking plugin development to the next level with plugin patterns: http://coding.smashingmagazine.com/2011/10/11/essential-jquery-plugin-patterns/.

Let's look at another plugin that helps you create those little boxes of information that come up when you hover over page elements: tooltips.

There is one tooltip plugin that's extremely flexible and easy to use while giving you absolute control over style, position, and even animation. It's called Tooltipsy and it's available from http://tooltipsy.com/.

One of the great things about Tooltipsy is that it offers a lot of options for styling and placing the tooltip in relation to the item being hovered over.

F The buttons on the GitHub site where you download Tooltipsy.

To install Tooltipsy:

1. Go to the website and click on the "Download Tooltipsy" link. That will take you to the GitHub site where you'll click on the Download .zip button **F**.

2. Save the zip file to your computer.

3. Extract the zip file to reveal the Tooltipsy files **G**.

4. Copy the **tooltipsy.min.js** file and place it into the **inc/jquery/** directory of your web server.

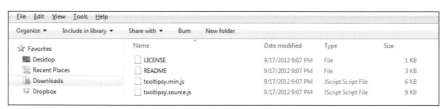

G The files included in the Tooltipsy download.

5. Create a new HTML file that includes all of the navigation elements as well as the floating menu (Script **10.3.html**). Save it as **tooltip.html** .

6. Include the Tooltipsy plugin by adding a script tag to the head section of **tooltip.html**. Make sure to include the plugin file after you've included the jQuery core file ⓘ.

The Tooltipsy plugin is now installed and ready to be used in your web page. You're going to add tooltips for the menu items in the floating menu.

Ⓗ The web page that you'll use the tooltips in.

```
<!-- JAVASCRIPT / JQUERY -->
<!--[if lt IE 9]>
    <script src="http://html5shim.googlecode.com/svn/trunk/html5.js"></script>
<![endif]-->
<script src="inc/jquery/jquery-1.7.2.js"></script>
<script src="inc/jquery/jcarousellite_1.0.1.js"></script>
<script src="inc/jquery/tooltipsy.min.js"></script>  ◄ • • • • • • • •
<script src="inc/jquery/jquery.custom.js"></script>
```

Ⓘ The placement of the script tag for the Tooltipsy plugin.

To use Tooltipsy in your web pages:

1. Modify the markup in **tooltip.html** to change the links in the floating menu (Script **10.3.html**). The changes are highlighted here:

```
<a href="7.5.html" class="hastip"
→title="Read the latest!">

Articles</a><br />

<a href="7.4.html" class="hastip"
→title="See our pics!">Photo
→Gallery</a><br />

<a href="7.3.html" class="hastip"
→title="Cook up something
→special!">Recipes</a><br />
```

2. Save the HTML file and upload it to your web server.

3. Create a function to attach Tooltipsy to the class assigned to the links:

```
$('.hastip').tooltipsy({
```

4. Begin assigning options by first setting the offset for the tooltip. The offset determines where the tooltip appears. These coordinates will be to the left of the link:

```
offset: [-10, 0],
```

5. Assign the remainder of the options, which in this case are the style properties for the tooltips. Once done, close out the brackets for the function:

```
css: {
    'padding': '5px',
    'max-width': '200px',
    'color': '#303030',
    'background-color':
    →'#f5f5b5',
    'border': '1px solid
    →#deca7e',
    '-moz-box-shadow': '0 0
    →10px rgba(0, 0, 0, .5)',
    '-webkit-box-shadow': '0 0
    →10px rgba(0, 0, 0, .5)',
    'box-shadow': '0 0 10px
    →rgba(0, 0, 0, .5)',
    'text-shadow': 'none'
}
});
```

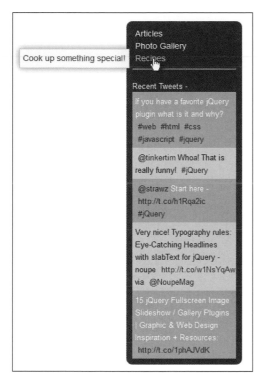

 Tooltips provide additional information to your website visitors.

6. Save **jquery.custom.js** and upload it to your web server.

7. Load the **tooltip.html** file into your browser and hover over the links in the floating menu to see the tooltips appear ❶.

The plugin takes the title attribute in each tag to use as the text for the tooltip. You can make that text as long as you'd like, and the tooltip will display it.

TIP **If you plan to use a lot of separate plugins in a website, you might consider concatenating all of the plugin code into one file to reduce server requests and increase performance.**

The ability to style the tooltips in the options is a real time-saver, too. The fact that you can put the CSS properties right in the call to the tooltip method will shorten your coding and development time. Make sure to check out some of the other options that Tooltipsy offers—you'll find some real jewels.

You can no doubt see the value of a well-written plugin in these examples, and you should know that there are thousands of jQuery plugins available on the web for nearly every facet of web development. When you find a plugin that you like, make sure that you examine its code to learn about JavaScript and jQuery coding practices and techniques that you can apply to your everyday development.

Rewind and Review

Take a few moments to reflect on what you've learned in this chapter:

- What three factors should govern your plugin choices?
- Why is good documentation essential for plugins?
- What kinds of things can you do with jQuery plugins?
- How are plugins typically installed in a web page?
- When using several plugins on a website, what can you do to increase performance?

11

Introducing jQuery UI

Perhaps the greatest collection of plugins for the jQuery library is jQuery's own UI (User Interface) library. Packed with effects and widgets, the jQuery UI library should be your first stop when you're looking for ways to enhance your websites and applications.

Many of the widgets in the jQuery UI library began their lives as plugins developed by independent developers just like you. As these plugins became more popular, they were rolled into the jQuery UI library to take advantage of optimizations available in the library's design. You'll find widgets for date pickers, tabs, and much more in jQuery UI. You'll also find a number of advanced animation effects. An advanced easing plugin is included with the core effects module.

Top that all off with the jQuery ThemeRoller, which lets you set any number of styles, including colors, fonts, and shadows. The ThemeRoller provides a number of ready-to-go themes, or you can roll your own before downloading the library. Let's get started with the ThemeRoller.

In This Chapter

Riding the ThemeRoller Coaster

One of the handiest features in the jQuery UI website (http://jqueryui.com) is the ThemeRoller. It allows you to easily set colors, fonts, shadows, and more for the widgets that you'll use in your websites .

If you don't want to customize the theme, you can pick from a wide array of pre-configured settings in the Theme Gallery. That's where we'll start our exercise for configuring, downloading, and installing the jQuery UI.

To configure the jQuery UI:

1. Open the jQuery UI website in your browser and click on the ThemeRoller.

2. Select the Gallery option at the top of the ThemeRoller .

3. Select the Start theme, as it closely matches the colors being used in the exercises. This allows you to preview the look of all the elements.

Ⓐ The jQuery UI ThemeRoller gives you plenty of options for matching style and design.

Ⓑ Several ready-made themes are yours to choose from.

4. Click the Download button just below the theme. This will take you to the page where you'll configure your options for the jQuery UI library 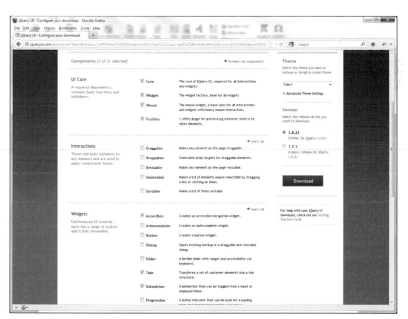.

5. Select the options that you'll need for the website that you're building. You'll only be using the tabs, accordion, and date picker in the current site. If you're unsure of the widgets that you'll be using, it's okay to select and download the entire library.

6. Select all of the options in the UI Core section. Without these, your widgets wouldn't work.

7. Click the Download button and save the compressed folder to your computer.

8. Extract all of the files to a folder on your system.

The jQuery library is now ready to be used; all you have to do is install it properly on your website. Several files are included in the download, but you'll need only a few of them for use on your website.

TIP A great way to learn the custom ThemeRoller is to take a website that you've designed or worked on and adjust the options in the ThemeRoller until you get a match for all of the styles in your website. Once you've completed your theme, save the configuration's URL from the website so that you can return to it if need be. The URL will contain a query string with all of your modifications.

TIP The styles you create in the Theme-wRoller can be used on any element in your website. Study the CSS generated to learn the style classes and then apply them to other elements in your websites to create a more unified look and feel. You can also get a comprehensive overview of the UI's class at http://api.jqueryui.com.

C The jQuery UI is highly customizable and allows you to download only the elements that you need.

To install the jQuery UI library:

1. Open the folder that you extracted the jQuery UI download in.

2. Copy the `jquery-ui-1.8.23.custom.min.js` and `jquery-1.8.0.min.js core` files (version 1.8.23 of the UI was the version available as of this writing; your version number may be different) from the `js/` folder and paste them into the same folder where your jQuery core library is located. The jQuery core file that ships with the download will be the latest compatible version of the jQuery core supporting the current UI version 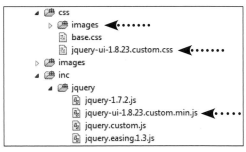.

3. Get the CSS for the UI library by copying the images folder and `jquery-ui-1.8.23.custom.css` from the `start/css/` directory in your extracted folder (Start is the name of the theme that you chose when configuring the library).

4. Paste both files into the directory where you have your CSS file ⓓ.

With the jQuery UI files in the proper place, you can go about including them in your HTML files.

ⓓ Be sure to place the jQuery UI files into the right location.

To include the jQuery UI files in your HTML:

1. Place a link tag for the jQuery UI CSS file in the head of your HTML document. Take the time to make sure that the path to the file is correct.

2. Place a script tag for the jQuery UI file in the head of your HTML file. The include for the jQuery UI file must come after the tag for the original jQuery core library.

Check again to make sure that the paths are correct and the jQuery UI library is ready to be used in your website **E**.

```
<!-- CSS -->
<link rel="stylesheet" href="css/base.css" />
<link rel="stylesheet" href="css/jquery-ui-1.8.23.custom.css" />   ◀······

<!-- JAVASCRIPT / JQUERY -->
<!--[if lt IE 9]>
    <script src="http://html5shim.googlecode.com/svn/trunk/html5.js"></script>
<![endif]-->
<script src="inc/jquery/jquery-1.7.2.js"></script>
<script src="inc/jquery/jquery-ui-1.8.23.custom.min.js"></script>   ◀······
<script src="inc/jquery/jquery.custom.js"></script>
```

E The markup to include the jQuery UI files gets everything ready for use.

Exploring Popular UI Widgets

Thanks to the extensive work by the jQuery team, adding widgets to your websites and applications couldn't be easier. In many cases, the HTML markup is the most extensive part of setting up of the jQuery widgets.

Each widget comes with several options to enhance its operation. (Be sure to read the documentation for each widget at http://jqueryui.com.) You'll have a lot of flexibility when it comes to picking and using options for the widgets, and each of the options is very easy to include.

Let's start the exploration of the jQuery UI widgets with one of the most popular widgets in use today: tabs.

To implement jQuery UI tabs:

1. Open the basic HTML page (Script **11.1.html**) with all navigation included in your text editor.

2. Place the following markup within the **div** with an **id** of **content**:

   ```
   <div id="tab_container">
   <ul>
   <li><a href="#tab1">Features</a>
   ⇢ </li>
   <li><a href="#tab2">
   Specification</a></li>
   <li><a href="#tab3">Reviews</a>
   ⇢ </li>
   </ul>
   ```

   The unordered list provides the text and navigation elements for the tabs.

3. Insert the **div**s that define each tab's content. You can place any markup that you'd like as content for a tab.

```
<div id="tab1">
<ul>
    <li>Looks great!</li>
    <li>Less fattening!</li>
    <li>Perfect for home or
    ↪ office!</li>
    <li>Reduces wrinkles!</li>
    <li>Available in a wide array
    ↪ of
    colors!</li>
</ul>
</div>
<div id="tab2">
</div>
<div id="tab3">
<p>This app does everything you
↪ could
possibly want it to do and not
↪ only
that, it is beautifully designed
↪ and
extremely intuitive to use.</p>
<p>Here are just some of the
fantastic reviews that we are
↪ very
humbled to say our app has
received:</p>
<ul>
    <li>I love this app, I
    ↪ couldn't
    be without it now.</li>
    <li>Where has this app been
    ↪ all
    my portable device owning
    life?</li>
    <li>It's official - my mobile
    device is complete!</li>
    <li>This app actually does
    everything it says and does
    ↪ it
    well, with style.</li>
</ul>
</div>
</div>
```

The second **div** has been intentionally left empty. You'll fill it with content later.

continues on next page

4. Save the file as **product.html** (Script **11.2.html**) and upload it to your web server. Load the page into your browser and you'll see all of the content **A**.

5. Open the **jquery.custom.js** file in your text editor and add the following line of jQuery code to bind the tabs function to the **div** containing your tab content:

`$('#tab_container').tabs();`

6. Save the file and upload it to your web server. Reload **product.html** in your web browser and you'll see that the content has been transformed **B**.

In this case, the markup was vastly more involved than the actual jQuery code to place the content into tabs. Take note that the links in the unordered list reference each **div**'s **id** attribute. The **id** in each **div** is what links the **div** to the navigation element in the unordered list.

`<a href="#tab1">`

The previous link references the **id** of this tab:

`<div id="tab1">`

Don't forget that a number of options are available for use with each jQuery UI widget. You'll see how to use the accordion next.

A All of the content is visible and the layout leaves something to be desired.

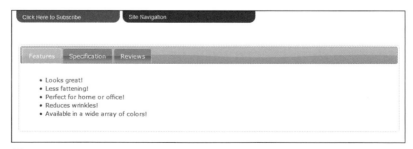

B The jQuery UI library takes care of the heavy lifting and turns plain old boring content into beautiful tabbed content.

To create a jQuery UI accordion:

1. Edit **product.html** (Script **11.3.html**) by placing the following markup in the second **div** of the tabs:

```
<div id="specifications">
<h3><a href="#">Weight &amp;
Dimensions</a></h3>
<div>
<ul>
    <li>Weight: 42kg</li>
    <li>Height: 27", Width: 41.3",
    Depth: 5.7"</li>
    <li>Shipping Weight: 61kg</li>
</ul>
</div>
<h3><a href="#">Inputs</a></h3>
<div>
<table>
<tr><td>HDMI Inputs</td>
    <td>2</td></tr>
<tr><td>USB Port</td>
    <td>Yes</td></tr>
<tr><td>USB Input</td>
    <td>Yes</td></tr>
<tr><td>DVI Inputs</td>
    <td>1</td></tr>
<tr><td>Component Video Inputs
→ </td>
    <td>2</td></tr>
<tr><td>Composite Inputs</td>
    <td>2</td></tr>
<tr><td>Media Card Slot</td>
    <td>No</td></tr>
</table>
</div>
<h3><a href="#">Accessories</a>
→ </h3>
<div>
<ul>
<li>Cargo Compartment Dress-Up
→ </li>
<li>Leather-Wrapped Shift Knob
→ </li>
<li>Illuminated Cup Holders</li>
<li>Sun Visors with Illuminated
Vanity Mirrors</li>
<li>Power Mirrors with Manual
Fold-Away</li>
<li>Remote Keyless Entry</li>
</ul>
</div>
<h3><a href="#">Shipping
Information</a></h3>
<div>
<p>Suspendisse eu nisl. Nullam ut
libero. Integer dignissim
→ consequat
lectus. Class aptent taciti
sociosqu
ad litora torquent per conubia
nostra, per inceptos himenaeos.
→ </p>
</div>
</div>
```

continues on next page

2. Save the file and upload it to your web server. After loading the page into your browser, you'll see the content in the second tab, Specification 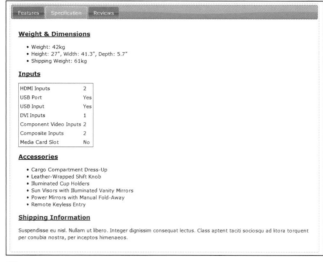.

3. Edit the **jquery.custom.js** file and include the function to add the accordion to the page:

```
$('#specifications').accordion({
    event: "mouseover"
});
```

You've added the option to use the **mouseover** event, which will animate each section of the accordion when the mouse hovers over a section header.

4. Save the jQuery file and upload it to your web server. Reload the **product. html** page, click the Specification tab, and you'll see the accordion 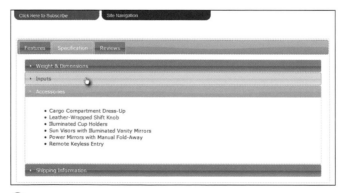.

C The new content is placed into the second tab.

D The accordion springs into action when you place the cursor over each header section.

You may have noticed a problem with your accordion. It may not be the full height needed to display the content 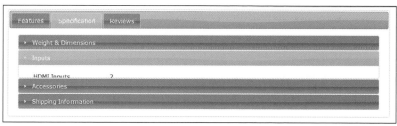.

If that's the case, it means you placed the accordion function after the tabs function. The tabs rendered before the accordion had a chance to finish. The fix is easy: Switch the order of the function calls, accordion first and then tabs. Doing so will allow the accordion to render first, giving the tabs function the information it needs to become the proper height for the content.

TIP When using jQuery UI widgets within the confines of another jQuery UI widget, order may matter when it comes to rendering each widget properly.

Once again, good markup is the key to the success of the function handling the content. The accordion homes in on the link reference prior to each **div** holding content within the accordion container.

Let's finish up the introduction to the jQuery UI by looking at another popular widget, the date picker. The options are more complex, but they'll make sense to you once you've finished the exercise.

To use the date picker widget:

1. Modify the recipe form page (Script **11.4.html**) to accept two dates: one for publishing the recipe and another to remove the recipe from publishing status. The markup for the affected area with the date inputs is highlighted here:

```
<p>Instructions</p>
<textarea
name="recipeInstructions">
</textarea><br />
<input type="text" name=
→ "publishDate"
placeholder="Date to Publish" />
<br />
<input type="text" name=
→ "removeDate"
placeholder="Date to Remove" />
<br />
<input type="submit" name="submit"
value="Submit Recipe" />
```

continues on next page

E Oops! Something has gone wrong in accordionville!

2. Save **recipe.html** and upload it to your web server .

3. Open **jquery.custom.js** in your text editor and begin the date picker function by binding the **datepicker()** widget to the first date input:

   ```
   $('input[name="publishDate"]')
   ```

   ```
   .datepicker({
   ```

   The earliest you want a recipe to be published is the day after it's submitted. Adding the option **minDate** with a value of **+1** solves that by making sure the calendar will only allow selections beginning tomorrow, based on the current system's date.

4. Add the option to start the calendar the day after the current system date:

   ```
   minDate: +1,
   ```

   You'll also want to make sure that the calendar choices for the second date picker come after the date from the first date picker (each recipe would then be published for a minimum of one day). The date picker widget has an event handler called **onSelect** in which you can define a function. The **onSelect** event handler is passed the selected date as an argument. The selected date can then be used to calculate a new date, which will be used to set the second date picker.

5. Make the **onSelect** function the second option of the date picker and create a variable to hold the date information from the selected date:

   ```
   onSelect: function(dateText) {
   ```

   ```
   var remove = new Date(dateText);
   ```

F The form inputs for the dates are in place.

Submit a recipe...

Recipe Name

Ingredients

Ingredient   change to spice
Ingredient   change to spice
Ingredient   add another ingredient

Instructions

Date to Publish

September 2012

Su Mo Tu We Th Fr Sa
                       1
2 3 4 5 6 7 8
9 10 11 12 13 14 **15**
16 17 18 19 20 21 22
23 24 25 26 27 28 29
30

G The first date input shows the calendar with tomorrow's date, provided today's date is September 14.

Submit a recipe...

Recipe Name

Ingredients

Ingredient   change to spice
Ingredient   change to spice
Ingredient   add another ingredient

Instructions

09/24/2012
Date to Remove

September 2012

Su Mo Tu We Th Fr Sa
                       1
2 3 4 5 6 7 8
9 10 11 12 13 14 15
16 17 18 19 20 21 22
23 24 **25** 26 27 28 29
30

H You can pick a date to stop publishing this recipe and know that it's in the future.

6. Calculate the starting date for the second date picker by adding one day to the currently selected date in the first date picker:

```
remove.setDate(remove.getDate()+1);
```

7. Apply the **minDate** option to the second date picker using the calculated date as its value and close out the brackets:

```
$('input[name="removeDate"]')
.datepicker({
    minDate: remove
});
}
});
```

8. Save **jquery.custom.js** and upload it to your web server. Reload **recipe.html** in your web browser and click or tab into the first date field **G**.

9. Select a publishing date, and then tab or click into the next date field. You'll see that the calendar starts on the day after the date that you originally selected **H**.

This is but one of the many options you'll have available to you when you choose to use the date picker widget in your projects.

Adding a Dialog Widget

Let's add one more widget to our form: a dialog box that the user has to acknowledge when they add a new ingredient field. Because you created a custom download of the jQuery UI library for the earlier exercises, you'll have to go back to the jQuery UI website, configure a new library, and then download and install the new library with the dialog widget included. Let's start there.

To install a new version of the jQuery library:

1. Return to the jQuery UI website and click the Download button in the site navigation **A**.

2. Select the Start theme from the drop-down box and make sure that all of the widgets are checked. Click the Download button to get the zip file containing the new library **B**.

A The download button is located in the primary navigation at http://jqueryui.com.

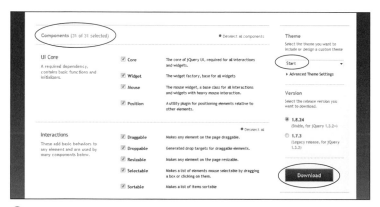

B Make sure that all of the widgets are selected, choose your theme, and click Download.

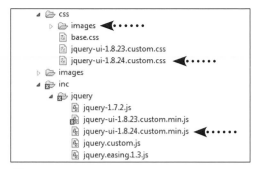

 C The files for the newly configured library are placed in the proper folders on the web server.

3. Copy the new files into the appropriate directories for the CSS and JavaScript files **C**. (As of this writing, the jQuery UI library had been upgraded to version 1.8.24. I left the previous version in the folder to support the earlier exercises.)

4. Open **recipe.html** (Script **11.5.html**) in your web browser and make changes to the tags that include the jQuery UI library's CSS and JavaScript files. Change the version numbers if appropriate **D**.

Now that you've got the reconfigured library installed, it's time to add the dialog box to the web page. The first thing that was done was modifying the CSS (**base.css**) file to make sure the dialog markup is hidden. Here's the rule that was added:

```
#recipe-dialog {
    display: none;
    font-size: .7em;
}
```

Now that the CSS has been modified, let's add the markup to the file and add the necessary jQuery function to enable the dialog box.

```
<!-- CSS -->
<link rel="stylesheet" href="css/base.css">
<link rel="stylesheet" href="css/jquery-ui-1.8.24.custom.css" />

<!-- JAVASCRIPT / JQUERY -->
<!--[if lt IE 9]>
    <script src="http://html5shim.googlecode.com/svn/trunk/html5.js"></script>
<![endif]-->
<script src="inc/jquery/jquery-1.7.2.js"></script>
<script src="inc/jquery/jquery-ui-1.8.24.custom.min.js"></script>
<script src="inc/jquery/jquery.custom.js"></script>
```

D Be sure to modify the link and script tags to reflect the proper files.

To add a jQuery UI dialog widget:

1. Modify **recipe.html** (Script **11.5.html**) in your text editor to include the following markup. Place the markup just before the closing body tag:

```
<div id="recipe-dialog" title="New
→ Ingredient">

<p>

    <span class="ui-icon
    → ui-icon-circle-check"
    → style="float:left; margin:
    → 0 7px 50px 0;"></span>

    You have added another
    → ingredient to your recipe.
    → Please make sure to fill
    → is out.

</p>

</div>
```

Note the span markup, which will include a check mark prior to the content in the dialog box **E**.

2. Save **recipe.html** and upload it to your web server.

3. Open **jquery.custom.js** in your text editor and find the function that you created to add ingredient fields to the form.

4. Modify the function by adding the following code block after the line in the function that reads:

```
$('input[name="recipeIngredient[]"]
→ ').filter(':last').focus();
```

Start by binding the selector for the recipe dialog to the **dialog()** method:

```
$('#recipe-dialog').dialog({
```

E The check mark icon has been added immediately before the content in the dialog box.

5. Set the options for the dialog box to make it a modal dialog and to include an acknowledgment button. Clicking OK will close the dialog and its modal overlay. Then close out the brackets for the dialog function:

```
modal: true,
buttons: {
    OK: function() {
        $( this ).dialog(
        ↪"close" );
    }
}
});
```

The jQuery UI dialog box offers a wide range of options that will allow you to create complex interactions when required.

6. Save the `jquery.custom.js` file and then upload it to your web server.

7. Load `recipe.html` into your browser and click on the "add another ingredient" link. The field will be added and the dialog box will be displayed **F**.

The jQuery UI library takes care of the styling of the modal dialog box as well as the modal overlay. Clicking the OK button closes the dialog and removes the overlay.

Now that you've gotten a small taste of the widgets and options available from the jQuery UI, be sure to go back to the site and try the other widgets and options available to you.

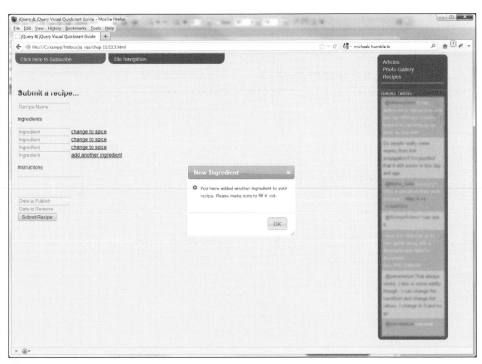

F The new dialog box appears when adding an ingredient field.

Rewind and Review

Take a few moments to reflect on what you've learned in this chapter:

- Do you need to have the jQuery core file in order to use the jQuery UI widget library?

- What three items from the compressed jQuery UI file must you have in order to ensure your widgets work?

- Can you customize a predefined theme in the jQuery UI ThemeRoller?

- If you're using easing with the jQuery UI, do you have to include a third-party plugin?

- In what order do you include the jQuery core and jQuery UI files?

- Which is usually more intensive: creating the markup for a widget or using the widget?

- Is more than one function available as an option for the date picker widget?

Fixing Common Problems

Learning anything new, especially a language like jQuery, comes with its fair share of mistakes and frustrations.

These little bumps in the road can range from small errors like writing selectors properly to having Ajax not return the proper information—or any information at all. Armed with the right tools and a little knowledge, you can typically solve these problems easily with little time lost to troubleshooting.

The focus here will be on identifying problems (many are identified in error messages provided by the browser) and then applying techniques to resolve the issues.

Nothing Works!

You've just created a web page and included your jQuery code, but when you load the page into your browser, none of the jQuery code you've written works. How do you search for the errors and correct them?

The first hint that something went wrong is an error indicator on the browser itself. Using the Firebug add-on with Firefox, you'll see an error count right away **Ⓐ**. Here's how to get more information about the errors.

To track down and fix a loading error:

1. Open the console of your web developer tools and search for the errors **Ⓑ**.

2. Identify the cause of the errors. In this case **jQuery** and the **$** alias for jQuery aren't defined, which means that the jQuery library didn't load. Confirm this by looking at the HTML tag. In Firebug you can expand the file reference to see the file's contents. In this exercise the jQuery core file reference isn't expandable.

3. Look closely at the defined path for the file. You'll see that there's a slash preceding the path where there shouldn't be **Ⓒ**.

4. Remove the slash from the script tag, and then save and reload the page. These errors should be gone!

If you've got similar errors for plugins, the troubleshooting steps are the same.

TIP Always make sure that you have the developer tools for your browser or another troubleshooting tool like Firebug installed and ready to go on your computer when developing jQuery code.

Ⓐ Oops! Something has gone wrong with our code.

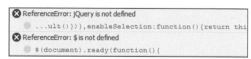

Ⓑ These errors tell you that jQuery didn't load.

```
<!DOCTYPE html>
<html lang="en">
  <head>
    <meta charset="utf-8">
    <title>jQuery & jQuery Visual Quickstart Guide</title>
    <meta content="" name="description">
    <meta content="" name="author">
    <link href="css/base.css" rel="stylesheet">
    <link href="css/jquery-ui-1.8.23.custom.css" rel="style
    <script src="/inc/jquery/jquery-1.7.2.js">
    <script src="inc/jquery/jquery-ui-1.8.23.custom.min.js"
    <script src="inc/jquery/jquery.custom.js">
1     /*
2      * name:          jquery.custom.js
3      * project:       jQuery & jQueryUI Visu
4      * author:        Jay Blanchard
5      */
6
7     $(document).ready(function(){
8             /* click to animate the registration o
9             $('$registration a').click(function(ev
```

Ⓒ The path to the jQuery core file has been mistyped.

TIP Some developers like to add an alert message or a `console.log` message immediately inside of the document ready handler during initial development. Either of these messages will be triggered if jQuery loads successfully. The alert or log messages can be removed once you're assured that jQuery is working.

A The form tells you that there's an error.

Nothing Comes Back from Ajax!

Using Ajax can raise the bar when it comes to creating errors and issues for developers. Problems can start at the browser with badly formed requests, path issues to the file you're trying to reach, and even database errors if the response is supposed to be dynamic.

Troubleshooting Ajax issues has to go a bit deeper because you'll need to have at least a basic knowledge of the server-side technology used, including any database system that might be in place. Your developer tool may not show any error counts on the surface.

It's important that your developer tool have a way to examine the request/response process when something does go wrong. For instance, the e-mail registration form has been filled out and submitted, and you know that you set the form to display a "Thank you" message when the request is successful. You were also smart enough to display a "Please resubmit!" message if something went wrong. That message is staring you in the face now **A**.

To troubleshoot the Ajax request:

1. Turn to your developer tool's console and locate the seemingly successful request that was made **B**.

2. Expand the request to find the response (Firebug has a Response tab) **C**.

   In this case it looks like the MySQL database is refusing connections. Check to make sure that the database is running.

If the database had been running you might have gotten another error, like one denying access to the database user **D**.

> **TIP** You must always test Ajax scripts on a working web server because the process expects to make an HTTP request to a URL. You can always install a web server on your development machine to assist you during development.

```
POST http://localhost/jq-vqs/chap-12/inc/php/registration.php   200 OK 4.05s
```

B The Ajax request looks like it was made properly.

```
POST http://localhost/jq-vqs/chap-12/inc/php/registration.php   200 OK 4.05s
    Headers   Post   Response   HTML
    <br />
    <b>Warning</b>:  mysql_connect() [<a href='function.mysql-connect'>function.mysql-connect</a>]: [2002
    ] No connection could be made because the target machine actively  (trying to connect via tcp://localhost
    :3306) in <b>C:\xampp\htdocs\jq-vqs\chap-12\inc\php\dbconnect.php</b> on line <b>11</b><br />
    <br />
    <b>Warning</b>:  mysql_connect() [<a href='function.mysql-connect'>function.mysql-connect</a>]: No connection
     could be made because the target machine actively refused it.
     in <b>C:\xampp\htdocs\jq-vqs\chap-12\inc\php\dbconnect.php</b> on line <b>11</b><br />
    No connection could be made because the target machine actively refused it.
```

C On closer examination, you see that it appears the database isn't running.

```
POST http://localhost/jq-vqs/chap-12/inc/php/registration.php   200 OK 39ms
    Headers   Post   Response   HTML
    <br />
    <b>Warning</b>:  mysql_connect() [<a href='function.mysql-connect'>function.mysql-connect</a>]: Access
     denied for user 'jq-vqs'@'localhost' (using password: YES) in <b>C:\xampp\htdocs\jq-vqs\chap-12\inc
    \php\dbconnect.php</b> on line <b>11</b><br />
    Access denied for user 'jq-vqs'@'localhost' (using password: YES)
    <br />
```

D The database is running, but the user isn't valid.

jQuery Doesn't Work in Ajax-Loaded Content

When loading dynamic content using Ajax, you'll find that the dynamically loaded elements won't react to jQuery code written for those elements.

The reason for that is because the newly loaded elements and the jQuery in the original page aren't aware of each other. The jQuery code for the original page has already run and has been bound to elements in the DOM that exists at the time the execution occurs.

The good news is that events occurring in the newly loaded content bubble up the DOM, including the DOM elements into which the jQuery is loaded **A**.

You can take advantage of the event bubbling by using jQuery's **on()** method. More specifically, you can use the method's delegation-style syntax.

With delegation you attach the **on()** method to a selector in the original markup where events in the dynamically loaded content will bubble up to. In many of the exercises in the book, a **div** with an **id="content"** was used to hold content loaded via Ajax **B**. Events from elements loaded into the **div** are delegated to that **div**.

```
<div id="content">  ◀ ············ bubbles up to here ◀ ···································
    <!-- content loaded via AJAX -->                                            ⋮
    <p>Send us your comments, we'd love to hear from you!</p>          a blur
    <p class="textInfo">You have typed <span>0</span> characters.</p>  event here
    <form name="contact" action="inc/php/contact.php" method="post">            ⋮
        <input type="text" name="contactName" placeholder="your name"/><span></span><br />
        <input type="text" name="contactEMail" placeholder= "your e-mail address"/><span></span><br /> ◀ ·····⋮
        <input type="text" name="contactPassword" placeholder="password not required" DISABLED/><span></span><br />
        <a href="" class="small_text" id="showPassword">Hide Password</a><br />
        <textarea name="contactComments" placeholder="your comments"></textarea><span></span><br />
        <select name="subscriberStatus">
            <option></option>
            <option value="non-subscriber">non-subscriber</option>
            <option value="subscriber">subscriber</option>
        </select><span></span><br />
        <button type="submit" name="submit">Send your comments</button>
    </form>
    <!-- end of AJAX content -->
</div>
```

A Events bubble up from dynamically loaded elements to those originally loaded before them.

```
<div class="pageWrapper">
    <!-- CONTENT -->
    <div id="content">
        <!-- content loaded via AJAX -->

        <!-- end of AJAX content -->
    </div>
    <div class="sidebar">
        <a href="7.5.html">Articles</a><br />
        <a href="7.4.html">Photo Gallery</a><br />
        <a href="7.3.html">Recipes</a><br />
        <hr />
        <div id="tweets">Recent Tweets - </div>
    </div>
</div>
```

B The markup for the content container in the original page.

To use the on() method with delegation:

1. Modify the jQuery code used to trigger an event handler to delegate it to an element that exists in the original DOM by selecting that element and attaching the **on()** method. Begin the **on()** method with the selector you want to handle in the dynamically loaded content:

    ```
    $('#content')
    .on('input[name="contactEMail"]',
    ```

2. Add the event handler that you wish to bubble up the DOM and then open the function call:

    ```
    'blur', function() {...
    ```

    The original selector and its binding looked like this:

    ```
    $('input[name="contactEMail"]')
    .blur(function() {...
    ```

    Now the jQuery should work on the dynamically loaded content for this event, because it bubbles up the DOM to an element that existed at the time the jQuery code was originally run.

Loading Two Libraries

If you've looked around, you know that there are other JavaScript libraries available for use in your websites. On occasion you might decide to use one of those libraries in addition to jQuery on your site. You go through the installation for both libraries; you write code for both libraries. Then you load the web page for the first time and you find that the effects for one library work while the effects for the other don't.

You might stumble upon changing the order in which the libraries load, placing one before the other in your web page **Ⓐ**. But now you find that the other set of effects works and the set that was working before doesn't.

What you're dealing with is a name space conflict. Both libraries are trying to use the same alias, in this case the **$**, to run their functions. Fortunately, there's an easy fix: the **jQuery.noConflict()** method. There are several ways to use the `noConflict()` method; the following is the easiest and quickest.

To use the jQuery. noConflict() method:

- Open your jQuery or JavaScript file in your text editor and modify your code to create a new namespace for jQuery.

```
$.noConflict();
jQuery(document).ready(
→ function($) {
    // Code that uses jQuery's $
    → can follow here.
});
    // Code that uses other
    → library's $ can follow here.
```

The loading order is not important at this stage; all you have to do is to make sure that you place all of your jQuery code in the document ready handler. Within the handler you can continue to use the **$** alias for all of your jQuery functions. This technique keeps you from having to rewrite code, which is especially convenient if you've already done a lot of development before you found the problem. Code for any other library can exist outside of the jQuery document ready handler.

```
<!-- JAVASCRIPT / JQUERY -->
<!--[if lt IE 9]>
    <script src="http://html5shim.googlecode.com/svn/trunk/html5.js"></script>
<![endif]-->
<script src="javascripts/scriptaculous.js" type="text/javascript"></script>  ◄••••••••••
<script src="inc/jquery/jquery-1.7.2.js"></script>  ◄•••••••••••
<script src="inc/jquery/jquery-ui-1.8.23.custom.min.js"></script>
<script src="inc/jquery/jquery.custom.js"></script>
```

Ⓐ Loading **Script.aculo.us** before loading jQuery.

As you grow in your jQuery development capabilities, you'll undoubtedly run into other problems that are more complex to identify and solve. Fortunately, there's a large community of jQuery developers who are online every day and are willing to help you troubleshoot issues and create solutions.

You can find help at the jQuery forums, http://forum.jquery.com, or at the programming question and answer site, http://stackoverflow.com/.

Rewind and Review

Take a few moments to reflect on what you've learned in this chapter:

- What is a handy little method for making sure the jQuery library has loaded?

- Where must you always test Ajax code?

- What is event delegation?

- Can you use more than one JavaScript library in your websites at the same time?

- What is the alias for jQuery?

- Where should you place code for libraries that are not jQuery?

- When an event moves up the DOM tree, what is it said to be doing?

- Is loading order important when using two or more different JavaScript libraries?

- Extra credit: Can an African swallow, a migratory bird, carry a coconut, a non-migratory fruit, over great distances?

jQuery vs. Other Technology

When it comes to JavaScript libraries, you won't find one that's more complete and intuitive than the jQuery library. But there may be times when you'll be looking for specific functionality not provided by the jQuery group of JavaScript libraries. This appendix provides information on the popular libraries available.

Dojo:
http://dojotoolkit.org

An extremely small and fast JavaScript library that supports DOM manipulation, events, effects, and animations.

Pros: Modules are individually loadable, giving you the ability to load only what you need to for any given web page. Supports AMD (Asynchronous Module Definition), which means that modules, including those by third parties supporting AMD, and the dependencies for those modules can be loaded asynchronously.

Cons: Managing module loads can be time-consuming and hard to document in larger websites. Syntax not as intuitive, especially given jQuery's CSS selector style.

YUI:
http://yuilibrary.com

A lightweight JavaScript and CSS library well suited for both desktop and mobile applications, built by front-end engineers at Yahoo.

Pros: Modular approach allows you to define actions needed on a page-by-page basis. Lots of modules to choose from, and the modules support DOM manipulation, event handling, and animations. Library also includes a number of "skins," which are similar to the jQuery UI widgets. Utilizes CSS selectors.

Cons: Module management can be unruly. Syntax is wordy and doesn't read cleanly.

Prototype:

http://prototypejs.org

A class-driven JavaScript library, based on classic object-oriented programming (OOP), that's aimed at DOM manipulation and Ajax functionality.

Pros: The library is very clean and focuses on providing specific functionality for DOM manipulation and for performing Ajax requests.

Cons: Requires external libraries for animations and effects (Script.aculo.us is the recommended add-on, available from http://script.aculo.us/). OOP methodology does not lend itself to a short learning curve.

MooTools:

http://mootools.net

Born from a plugin originally released for Prototype, the MooTools library has grown into a full-fledged modular, lightweight JavaScript library. It includes components for enhancing JavaScript natives, creating effects, performing Ajax requests, and manipulating CSS.

Pros: The library has a modular approach, allowing you to load only what you need. It's extremely extensible, allowing you to create new and useful functionality.

Cons: Documentation is scarce and lacks good tutorials. Online third-party tutorials are older and not useful with updates to the library.

ExtJS:

http://www.sencha.com/products/extjs

ExtJS was originally built as an add-on for the YUI library and has eventually become part of the product line for a company called Sencha. It's a library more along the lines of jQuery UI—it features widgets and includes animation and drawing packages. Perhaps its best feature is the charting package that you can use right out of the box.

Pros: Built-in widgets for creating compelling charts. Provides a lot of choices for using and configuring widgets.

Cons: Extensive licensing options, but commercial options are not free. Documentation is extensive but can be difficult to understand for those new to JavaScript.

These are only a few of the JavaScript libraries available on the web today. There are also some highly specialized libraries that focus on particular actions that you can perform with JavaScript, like effects, Ajax, form validation, and charting. Many of these can be found at the website http://javascriptlibraries.com.

An Active jQuery Website

As you learn to develop with jQuery, you'll find that code organization, documentation, and readability should be first and foremost when it comes to putting your websites and web applications together.

This appendix can be your guide to keeping things straight as well as giving you a starting point for any web project you might create with jQuery, HTML5, and CSS.

You'll also find the information for laying out downloadable code examples available from www.jayblanchard.net.

HTML5 Boilerplate

Two examples are provided: one is really basic and includes the use of the Google CDN, and the other is a fallback in the event the CDN is not available. Here's the markup for the basic template (Script `basic_html5.html`):

```
<!DOCTYPE html>

<html>

<head>

    <!-- BASIC INFORMATION -->

    <meta charset="UTF-8">

    <title>insert title here</title>

    <!-- CSS -->

    <!-- JAVASCRIPT / JQUERY -->

    <script type="text/javascript"
    → src="https://ajax.googleapis.
    → com/ajax/libs/jquery/1.7.2/
    → jquery.min.js">

    </script>
```

code continues on next page

```
<script type="text/javascript">
if (typeof jQuery ==
→ 'undefined') {

document.write(unescape
→ ("%3Cscript
→ src='inc/jquery-1.7.2.min.js'
→ type='text/javascript'%3E%3C/
→ script%3E"));

}

</script>
```

```
</head>
<body>
    <!-- CONTENT -->
</body>
</html>
```

The basic template is good for small projects and to learn how to integrate jQuery into your web projects. The DOCTYPE declaration at the top of the page is correct for all HTML5.

The more robust template (Script **html5_boilerplate.html**) includes some conditional statements that will take care of issues with various versions of Microsoft's Internet Explorer browser. The markup also includes a reference to a CDN version of an HTML5 shim that will assist Internet Explorer versions before 9 in rendering and using HTML5 markup correctly.

```
<!DOCTYPE html>
<!--[if lt IE 7 ]><html class="ie ie6"
→ lang="en"> <![endif]-->
<!--[if IE 7 ]><html class="ie ie7"
→ lang="en"> <![endif]-->
<!--[if IE 8 ]><html class="ie ie8"
→ lang="en"> <![endif]-->
```

```
<!--[if (gte IE 9)|!(IE)]><!--><html
→ lang="en"> <!--<![endif]-->
<head>

    <!-- BASIC INFORMATION -->
    <meta charset="utf-8">
    <title>insert page title</title>
<meta name="description" content="">
    <meta name="author" content="">


    <!-- CSS -->


    <!-- JAVASCRIPT / JQUERY -->
    <!--[if lt IE 9]>
<script src="http://html5shim.
→ googlecode.com/svn/trunk/html5.js">
→ </script>
    <![endif]-->
<script type="text/javascript"
→ src="https://ajax.googleapis.com/
→ ajax/libs/jquery/1.7.2/jquery.
→ min.js"></script>

<script type="text/javascript">
if (typeof jQuery =='undefined'){
→ document.write(unescape("%3Cscript
→ src='inc/jquery-1.7.2.min.js'
→ type='text/javascript'%3E%3C/
→ script%3E"));
    }
    </script>


</head>
<body>
    <!-- CONTENT -->
</body>
</html>
```

```
▷ 🗁 chap-1
▷ 🗁 chap-2
▷ 🗁 chap-3
▷ 🗁 chap-4
▲ 🗁 chap-5
   ▲ 🗁 css
         📄 base.css
   ▷ 🗁 images
   ▲ 🗁 inc
      ▲ 🗁 jquery
            📄 jquery-1.7.2.js
            📄 jquery.custom.js
         🗁 php
      📄 5.1.html
      📄 5.2.html
      📄 5.3.html
      📄 5.4.html
▷ 🗁 chap-6
▷ 🗁 chap-7
▷ 🗁 chap-8
▷ 🗁 chap-9
▷ 🗁 chap-10
▷ 🖿 chap-11
▷ 🗁 chap-12
▷ 🗁 chap-appendix-b
```

A The download contains the code for each chapter. Chapter 5 is shown expanded so that you can see the organization.

Download the Code

The code for all of the exercises as well as the HTML5 boilerplate examples are available for download from www.jayblanchard.net.

Each chapter stands alone in as much as it includes the jQuery files, CSS, and markup to work independently of code for other chapters.

The layout of the download is done by chapter **A**.

Feel free to download and use the latest version of jQuery (version 1.8.2 was available as of this writing) from http://jquery.com/download/. All of the examples will work with the newer versions. Version 1.7.2 was used to develop all of the exercises and is included in the download from www.jayblanchard.net.

The jQuery code in **jquery.custom.js** was developed as the book progressed and is updated in each **inc/jquery/** directory as each chapter progresses.

PHP and MySQL

Three files are used to support the Ajax interaction in Chapter 7, "Using Ajax." One is the PHP file that handles the registration request. The other PHP file is the one used to set up the connection to a MySQL database. The last file is a SQL file used to set up the table in your database that will hold the e-mail addresses.

registration.php

```php
<?php
/* database connection */
include 'dbconnect.php';

/* insert email address into
  database */
$userEMail = mysql_real_escape_
  string($_POST['userEMail']);

if('' != $userEMail) {
$sql = "INSERT INTO
  `jqvqs`.`registeredemail`(`address`)
  VALUES('" . $userEMail ."')";

if(!$result = mysql_query($sql,
  $dbc)) {
    /* there is a problem */
    echo mysql_error() . "\n";
} else {
    /* the insert was a success */
    echo 1;
}
}
?>
```

dbconnect.php

```php
<?php
// change the user and password if
  needed
$user = 'jqvqs';
$pass = 'jqueryrocks';


if(!$dbc = mysql_connect('localhost',
  $user, $pass)) {
    echo mysql_error() . "\n";
}
?>
```

create_registration.sql

```sql
CREATE TABLE IF NOT EXISTS
`registeredemail` (
    `id` int(11) NOT NULL
    AUTO_INCREMENT,
    `address` varchar(256) NOT NULL,
    PRIMARY KEY (`id`)
) ENGINE=InnoDB  DEFAULT
  CHARSET=latin1 AUTO_INCREMENT=1 ;
```

A discussion of how to set up a PHP server and MySQL database is beyond the scope of this book, but you can download packages that will allow you to easily set up a web server on your desktop that includes PHP and MySQL. Windows users, visit www.apachefriends.org/en/xampp.html. Mac users, you can use XAMPP or visit www.mamp.info/en/index.html, where you can download and install the MAMP web server package. Both packages are easy to install and configure and have great community support.

Index

Symbols

{} (curly brackets), using with attributes, 49

" (quotes), using with attribute selectors, 82

A

accordion widget, 169–171

:active CSS pseudo-class selectors, 7

add() DOM tree traversal method, 103

addClass() function, 36, 50–51

    usage, 36

    using, 50–51

:after CSS pseudo-class selectors, 7

after() DOM insertion manipulator, 56

AJAX (Asynchronous JavaScript and XML). *See also* JSON (JavaScript Object Notation)

    attaching on() method, 117–119

    event bubbling, 117–118

    execution of requests, 110

    get() shorthand method, 110

    getJSON() shorthand method, 110, 123–125

    getScript() shorthand method, 110

    load() shorthand method, 110–116

    managing loaded content, 117–118

AJAX *(continued)*

    PHP and MySQL, 120

    post() shorthand method, 110, 119–121

    shorthand methods, 110

    testing server-side scripts, 121

Ajax requests, troubleshooting, 181–182

Ajax scripts, testing, 182

all selector, 2, 4

alt attribute, using, 47

andSelf() DOM tree traversal method, 103

animate() custom animation method, 133, 135–139

animations, easing, 130. *See also* custom animation methods

append() DOM insertion manipulator, 56, 58–60

appendTo() DOM insertion manipulator, 56, 60–61

applications, planning, xix

arguments

    explained, xii–xiv

    passing to functions, xiv

    transformation of, xiv

    as windows, 142

DOM CSS manipulators *(continued)*

    setting measurements, 69–71

    `unwrap()` method, 57

    `width()` method, 57, 62–65

    `wrap()` method, 57

    `wrapAll()` method, 57

    `wrapInner()` method, 57

DOM elements

    checking, 142

    sorting array of, 142

    storing data on, 146–149

DOM insertion manipulators

    `after()`, 56

    `append()` method, 56, 58–60

    `appendTo()` method, 56, 60–61

    `before()`, 56, 67–68

    `clone()`, 56

    `detach()`, 56

    `empty()`, 56

    `insertAfter()`, 56

    `insertBefore()`, 56

    `prepend()`, 56

    `prependTo()`, 56

    rearranging order, 67–68

    `remove()`, 56

    `removeAfter()`, 56

    `replaceAll()`, 56

    `replaceWith()`, 56

    `unwrap()`, 56

    `wrap()`, 56

    `wrapAll()`, 56

    `wrapInner()`, 56

DOM nodes

    as XML documents, 142

    in XML documents, 142

DOM tree event bubbling, 117–118

DOM tree traversal filters

    `eq()`, 102–106

    `filter()`, 102

    `first()`, 102

    `has()`, 102

    `is()`, 102

    `last()`, 102

    `map()`, 102–103

    `slice()`, 102, 106–107

DOM tree traversal methods

    `add()`, 103

    `andSelf()`, 103

    `children()`, 96

    `closest()`, 96, 100–101

    `contents()`, 103

    `end()`, 103

    `find()`, 96, 99–100

    `next()`, 96–98

    `nextAll()`, 96

    `nextUntil()`, 96

    `not()`, 103

    `offsetparent()`, 96

    `parent()`, 96, 98

    `parents()`, 96

    `parentsUntil()`, 96

    `prev()`, 96–97

    `prevAll()`, 96

    `prevUntil()`, 96

    `siblings()`, 96

E

easing animations, 130

Eclipse IDE, described, xx, 3

`element` selector, 2

elements, looping through, 143–145

`:empty` CSS pseudo-class selectors, 7

empty() DOM insertion manipulator, 56

empty function, indicating, 142

:enabled CSS pseudo-class selectors, 7

end() DOM tree traversal method, 103

eq() DOM tree traversal filter, 102–106

event bubbling. *See also* troubleshooting

    explained, 117–118

    using with Ajax-loaded content, 183

event handlers. *See also* form event handlers;
    keyboard events; mouse events

    attaching, 16

    ready(), 16

ExtJS versus jQuery, 188

F

fadeIn() visibility method, 128

fadeOut() visibility method, 128

fadeTo() visibility method, 128

FadeToggle() visibility method, 128

filter() DOM tree traversal filter, 102

filter() method, using, 8

filters

    :animated, 6

    applying to selectors, 6–7

    content type, 9

    :eq(), 6

    :even, 6, 11–12

    extensions, 6, 10

    :first, 6

    :gt(), 6

    :has(), 6

    :header, 6

    :hidden, 6

    :lt(), 6

    :[name!="value"], 6

    :odd, 6, 11–12

filters *(continued)*

    :parent, 6

    :selected, 6

    using, 8

    :visible, 6

find() DOM tree traversal method, 96,
    99–100

Firebug, described, xx

first() DOM tree traversal filter, 102

:first-child CSS pseudo-class selectors, 7

:first-letter CSS pseudo-class selectors, 7

:first-line CSS pseudo-class selectors, 7

floating menu, creating, 69–71

:focus CSS pseudo-class selectors, 7

focus() form event handler, 30

focusout() method, using, 28–29

for condition, using, xiii

form elements

    disabling with prop() function, 40–41

    enabling with prop() function, 40–41

form event handlers. *See also* event handlers

    blur(), 30–32

    change(), 30, 32–33

    focus(), 30

    select(), 30

    submit(), 30

    test() method, 32

forms, changing input elements, 76–79

functions. *See also* methods

    empty, 142

    executing on queues, 142

    explained, xiii

    versus methods, xiv

    naming, xiii

    showing queue for execution, 142

    using, xiv

G

GitHub site, accessing for Tooltipsy, 156

Google Closure Compiler, minifying code with, xviii–xix

H

`has()` DOM tree traversal filter, 102

`hasClass()` function, 36, 52

`height()` method, 57, 62–65

`hide()` visibility method, 128–129

`:hover` CSS pseudo-class selectors, 7

`hover()` method

    functions, 23

    `hover()`, 22

    navigation elements, 23

    usage, 19

    using, 22

HTML5 boilerplate, 189–190

I

ID attribute, explained, 2

`id` selector, 2

`innerHeight()` method, 57

`innerWidth()` method, 57

input

    getting value with `val()`, 43–44

    setting value with `val()`, 43

input elements, changing, 76–79

input type, changing via `prop()`, 38–39

`insertAfter()` DOM insertion manipulator, 56

`insertBefore()` DOM insertion manipulator, 56

installing

    jCarousel Lite, 152–153

    jQuery UI library, 164

    Tooltipsy, 156

`is()` DOM tree traversal filter, 102

iterating over objects and arrays, 142

J

JavaScript code, executing globally, 142

JavaScript Object Literals, 49

jCarousel Lite. *See also* plugins

    installing, 152–153

    using, 154–156

jQuery

    arguments, xii–xiv

    described, xii

    versus Dojo library, 187

    downloading, xvi–xvii, 191

    versus ExtJS library, 188

    functions, xiii

    learning, xii

    versus MooTools library, 188

    versus Prototype library, 188

    using in projects, xvii

    variables, xii–xiv

    versus YUI library, 187

jQuery library, installing version of, 174–175

jQuery methods

    caching selectors, 75

    chaining, 75

jQuery UI

    configuring, 162–163

    ThemeRoller, 162

    website, 162

jQuery UI files, including in HTML, 165

jQuery UI library, installing, 164

jQuery UI widgets

    accordion, 169–171

    date picker, 171–173

    dialog, 174–177

    implementing tabs, 166–168

    order of, 171

`jQuery.*()` utility methods, 142

`jquery.custom.js` file, saving, 21

N

[name*="value"] selector, finding substrings with, 83–85

[name~=value] selector, using, 85–88

[name!=value] selector, using, 89–90

next() DOM tree traversal method, 96–98

nextAll() DOM tree traversal method, 96

nextUntil() DOM tree traversal method, 96

noConflict() method, using with libraries, 185–186

not() DOM tree traversal method, 103

not equal selector
described, 82
using, 88–90

:not(selector) CSS pseudo-class selectors, 7

:nth-child(n) CSS pseudo-class selectors, 7, 12

:nth-last-child(n) CSS pseudo-class selectors, 7

O

objects. *See also* array-like objects
determining empty status of, 142
iterating over, 142
merging contents of, 142
plain type, 142
returning from JSON string, 142

offset() method, 57, 69–71
DOM CSS manipulators, 69–71
usage, 57

offsetparent() DOM tree traversal method, 96

on() method
using with delegation, 183–184
using with lightbox effect, 66

:only-child CSS pseudo-class selectors, 7

outerHeight() method, 57

outerHTML() helper function custom animation method, 134

outerWidth() method, 57

P

parent() DOM tree traversal method, 96, 98

parents() DOM tree traversal method, 96

parentsUntil() DOM tree traversal method, 96

password
error message, 44
form field for, 38
visibility, 39

password field, enabling, 41

photo gallery
setting titles for pictures, 47
starting point for, 46

PHP and MySQL
dbconnect.php file, 192
registration.php file, 192
using, 120

plugin code, concatenating, 158

plugins. *See also* jCarousel Lite
creating, 155
download options, 152
looking for, 152
Tooltipsy, 156

position() method, 57

prepend() DOM insertion manipulator, 56

prependTo() DOM insertion manipulator, 56

prev() DOM tree traversal method, 96–97

prevAll() DOM tree traversal method, 96

prevUntil() DOM tree traversal method, 96

problems. *See* troubleshooting

Products tables, 144–145

progressive enhancement, performing, xix

prop() function, 36
    versus attr() method, 39
    disabling form elements, 40–41
    enabling form elements, 40–41
    using to change input type, 38–39
properties
    changing, 37–42
    removeProp() function, 41–42
Prototype versus jQuery, 188

Q

queue, removing items from, 142
queue() custom animation method, 133
quotes ("), using with attribute selectors, 82

R

ready() handler
    execution of, 16
    relationship to DOM elements, 18
    using in separate files, 17
    using in web pages, 18
rearranging order DOM insertion manipulator,
    67–68
recipe form
    changing ingredients, 100
    creating, 73
registration.php file, 192
regular expressions, 32
remove()
    DOM insertion manipulator, 56
    method, 57, 66
removeAfter() DOM insertion manipulator, 56
removeAttr() function, 36, 57
removeClass() function, 36, 51–52
    usage, 36
    using, 51–52

removeProp() function, 36, 41–42
replaceAll()
    DOM insertion manipulator, 56
    method, 57
replaceWith()
    DOM insertion manipulator, 56
    method, 57, 76–79
:root CSS pseudo-class selectors, 7

S

scrollLeft() method, 57
scrollTop() method, 57, 69–71
select() form event handler, 30
selectors. *See also* attribute selectors;
    CSS pseudo-class selectors
    all, 2, 4
    applying filters to, 6–7
    attribute type, 12–13
    caching, 4, 75
    class, 2
    combining, 5, 91–93
    element, 2
    id, 2
    improving performance, 4
    not equal, 82, 88–90
    using, 3–4
server-side scripts, testing, 121
show() visibility method, 128–129
siblings() DOM tree traversal method, 96
slice()
    DOM tree traversal filter, 102, 106–107
    traversal method, 10
stop()method, 23, 133
stored data values, getting, 148–149.
    See also data
storing data, 142
strings, parsing into XML documents, 142

Sublime Text 2, described, xx

`submit()` form event handler, 30

substrings, finding, 83–85

T

tabs, implementing with jQuery UI, 166–168

`test()` method form event handler, 32

ThemeRoller

    described, 162

    learning, 163

    use of styles, 163

`this` versus `$(this)`, 14

time, returning number for, 142

`toggle()` method, 23, 128–130

`toggleClass()` function, 36, 53

    usage, 36

    using, 53

tools

    Developer Tools, xx

    Eclipse IDE, xx

    Firebug, xx

    MAMP, xx

    Sublime Text 2, xx

    XAMPP, xx

Tooltipsy

    installing, 156

    using in web pages, 157–159

troubleshooting. *See also* event bubbling

    Ajax requests, 181–182

    Ajax-loaded content, 183–184

    loading errors, 180

    loading libraries, 185–186

    using `noConflict()` method, 185–186

    using `on()` method with delegation, 183–184

tweets, hiding and showing, 129

U

UI (User Interface). *See* jQuery UI

`unwrap()`method,56–57

utilities website, 141

utility methods

    getting data, 146–149

    `jQuery.data()`, 146–149

    `jQuery.each()`, 143–145, 147

    letter case, 145

    setting data, 146–149

    table of, 142

V

`val()` function

    usage, 36

    using, 43–44

values, managing, 43–44

variables

    explained, xii–xiv

    naming, xiii

visibility methods

    easing plugin, 130

    `fadeIn()`, 128

    `fadeOut()`, 128

    `fadeTo()`, 128

    `FadeToggle()`, 128

    `hide()`, 128–129

    `show()`, 128–129

    `toggle()`, 128–130

`:visited` CSS pseudo-class selectors, 7

W

websites

    building, 16

    code for chapters, xii, 191